MAKE A
DIFFERENCE
AT WORK

OVER 500 WAYS TO
MAKE THE ENVIRONMENT
YOUR BUSINESS

THINK
BOOKS

First published in Great Britain by Think Books in 2008
This edition published in 2008 by Think Books,
an imprint of Pan Macmillan Ltd
Pan Macmillan, 20 New Wharf Road, London N1 9RR
Basingstoke and Oxford
Associated companies throughout the world
www.panmacmillan.com
www.think-books.com

ISBN: 978-1-84525-050-8

Text Copyright: Pan Macmillan Ltd
Design Copyright: Think Publishing

Author: Adharanand Finn
Designer: James Collins
Think Books: Tania Adams, Caroline Grogan, Emma Jones, Caitlin Mackesy Davies,
Jackie Scully, Mark Searle, Marion Thompson and Charlie Nutbrown.

1 3 5 7 9 8 6 4 2 1

A CIP catalogue record for this book is available from the British Library.

Printed in Italy by Printer Trento S.r.l

Visit www.panmacmillan.com to read more about all our books and to buy
them. You will also find features, author interviews and news of any
author events, and you can sign up for e-newsletters so that you're
always first to hear about our new releases.

Cover image and design: Bishbo

Mixed Sources
Product group from well-managed
forests and other controlled sources
www.fsc.org Cert no. CQ-COC-000012
© 1996 Forest Stewardship Council

The paper used for this book has been independently certified as having
been sourced from well-managed forests and recycled wood or fibre
according to the rules of the Forest Stewardship Council.

This book has been printed and bound in Italy by Printer Trento S.r.l.,
an FSC-certified company for printing books on FSC mixed paper in
compliance with the chain of custody and on products labelling standards.

Thanks

This book has only been made possible with the help and enthusiastic support of many organisations and individuals, and our thanks go to:

BTCV, CTC, Department for Transport, Edward Bulmer, Natural Collection, Forum for the Future, Friends of the Earth, Responsibletravel.com, Surfers against Sewage, Sustrans, Timebank, Tony Juniper and Jonathon Porritt.

We would also like to thank all of the advertisers who have supported this book.

Contents

Foreword

Many of us spend more time in the office than at home. So while we're getting used to recycling and saving energy around the house, we might still be wasting lots of resources at work.

Businesses may be big consumers – leaving lights on all weekend, using vast amounts of paper and constantly upgrading equipment – but there's huge scope for change. Friends of the Earth believes we can all do our bit to make a difference – at work, at home, on our travels – but things don't just happen, we make them happen. And the more of us that make changes, the greater the impact we'll have.

A good starting point is good information. Businesses are becoming aware that reducing their impact on the environment can have financial and reputation gains too: and bigger changes will have a bigger impact. But a business doesn't go green on its own – it takes leadership from business owners and managers, as well as an enthusiastic response from staff.

Good office management can really improve efficiency through improvements such as insulation and double-glazing, to easy steps like setting printers to using both sides of the paper. Even turning off your monitor when you leave your desk even for 10 minutes, and encouraging 20 others to do the same, can save one tonne of carbon dioxide emissions in an hour – employees who leave their computers on overnight cost their companies £90 million in 2002. What's more, those computers pumped 2.8 million tonnes of carbon dioxide into the environment.

Lots of small changes really do add up. No matter what your job, there are things that you can do to make your workplace more planet friendly. Read on to find out how you can make a difference.

Tony Juniper
Executive Director, Friends of the Earth

WWW.
ECOTOPIA.
CO.UK

Make a difference
www.ecotopia.co.uk
Environmental and socially responsible shopping

Introduction

I hardly meet anybody these days who believes that a 'business as usual' approach to creating wealth is any longer 'fit for purpose'. There are just so many environmental and social issues clamouring for urgent and serious attention. But the problem is that a lot of the advocacy around avoiding 'business as usual' is very downbeat – much too much along the lines of 'adapt or die' rather than 'adapt and thrive'. This downbeat characterisation is obviously buried fairly deep in the national psyche – and even deeper in the psyche of most UK companies, for whom the environmental agenda has always been one of cost and regulatory hassle – as in 'if you don't get this sorted, you're going down!'.

Human nature being what it is, and corporate interests being what they are, I'd so much rather press the 'help the planet, help yourself' button! So that's one of the reasons why I hope this hands-on and very helpful book really prospers, not least by reaching the parts of the business system that everybody knows are the hardest to reach – namely the small and medium-sized enterprises, but the millions of micro-enterprises on which our future economic success totally depends.

There is a school of thought that would have us believe that 'everyone can be a winner' as we move towards a more sustainable, low-carbon economy. Rubbish! There will, in that time-honoured way in any capitalist economy, be winners and losers. And the business winners, however big or small they may be, will be those that understand that energy, carbon, waste, water, materials, community involvement, supply chain management and staff motivation are now all central to business success – not just a nice 'add-on'.

Awareness is one thing. Real business leadership means finding the time and the resources to start doing the basics – and there's no better place to start that than with the wise words of advice here in *Make a Difference at Work*.

Jonathon Porritt
Founder Director, Forum for the Future

The Working Week

The ETA - Your green breakdown cover provider

Until there's a better way let's make driving greener.

Your green
peace of mind

3 months FREE
quote
1923 7013

The ETA - Your green breakdown cover provider

The ETA is the world's only climate neutral motoring organisation, providing an ethical first class breakdown cover at competitive rates.

As well as encouraging responsible driving to reduce carbon, the ETA helps drivers neutralise their impact on global warming, and funds many projects on the developing world. The ETA is a not-for-profit organisation, meaning that your money goes back into providing you with the best breakdown service possible and the best future for this planet.

With over 15 years experience, 80% success rate of fixing vehicles roadside and a national network of over 1700 repair and recovery agents you can relax, you are in safe han,ds.

So go on, join the ETA today!

0800 212 810
www.eta.co.uk

Why join the ETA

- Funding green projects around the world
- 85% of vehicles repaired at roadside
- Average call out time of 40 mins
- World's only climate neutral motoring organisation
- National network of 1,700 repair and rescue agents
- Discounts on ethical carbon neutral Home, Car and Holiday Insurance
- Bi-monthly E magazine
- Over 15 years experience
- Bi-monthly newsletter

The ETA - The world's only climate neutral motoring organisation

Monday morning

In the short time between getting up and leaving the house, the potential for environmental damage is huge. All across the country every Monday morning lights go on, showers and baths pour out hot water, harmful chemicals are doused liberally all over the place – from toothpastes to deodorants – kettles boil too much water; it's like a chemical and emissions waste-fest. The good news is that tackling it doesn't necessarily mean getting up earlier. In most cases, a few simple changes can make a big difference. For example, putting just one aluminium can in the recycling box instead of the bin can save enough energy to keep your television running for three hours, while hanging out one load of washing each week, instead of using the tumble dryer, could save up to 515,000 tonnes of CO_2 emissions in a year – to offset that amount of carbon dioxide you would need to plant over 12 million hardwood saplings. So, make a change on the hardest morning of the week and you're off to a good start.

Breakfast

YOUR EMISSIONS ARE WHAT YOU EAT Green campaigner and Green Party candidate Chris Goodall recently courted controversy by suggesting that walking to the shops could be more environmentally damaging than driving. Although this is a dubious statement, to say the least, it was intended to raise the valid point that our food production often gets overlooked when it comes to our environmental concerns. His conclusion was based on the fact that the environmental cost of producing enough beef to give you the energy to walk to the shop would cause more damage to the planet than the car journey. Of course, no one eats only beef, and even sitting in your car requires energy, but it is an interesting point. Your choice of food can have a huge effect on your environmental impact. Providing you with 10 litres of orange juice, for example, requires one litre of fuel for processing and transportation to the UK, and 220 litres of water for irrigation and cleaning. Then there are those hard-to-recycle cartons it usually comes in. So, choose your food carefully. Choose locally produced, organic food. Choose farmers' markets. Choose less meat. Choose seasonal produce. There is a whole world of information out there on the eco-diet, but a good place to start if you want more information is the Soil Association (www.soilassociation.org).

EAT SEASONAL PRODUCE All fruits and vegetables, and even meat and fish to a lesser extent, have seasonal lifecycles. Vast amounts of land on the other side of the world have been taken over to provide us with strawberries in the winter and satsumas during summer. Local, seasonal produce tastes better, costs less and saves on food miles. Find out more from **www.eattheseasons.co.uk**.

VISIT A FARMERS' MARKET Buying direct from the farmer cuts out the middleman, meaning the food has to travel less, creating fewer emissions. It is also fresher, fewer shops have to be lit and heated or cooled, the food is cheaper and the farmer gets a better deal. If it's an organic farmers' market, then that's even better. To find your local farmers' market and to find local farm shops, visit **www.bigbarn.co.uk**.

GET A VEGETABLE BRUSH One thing that puts people off buying seasonal, organic veg from the local farmer is the fact that often it is covered in mud. If the effort of cleaning off all that dirt leaves you longing for polished, supermarket produce, you need to invest a few pounds in a vegetable brush. The Natural Collection (**www.naturalcollection.com**), for example, sells a nice wooden one.

GET A HOME DELIVERY While walking to your local shop and buying fresh, organic, local produce is almost certainly the greenest way to shop, for many of us this is not possible – either you don't have a local shop, or it only sells crisps and sweets. So, instead, you hop in your car and drive to the supermarket. Online shopping, however, takes the hopping in the car part out of the equation. Online supermarkets, such as Tesco.com or Ocado.com, give you the same choice as the big supermarket stores, but deliver it to your door for the ultimate in convenience. And the green bit? According to Ocado's chief operating officer, each delivery van replaces 20 car journeys. Most services will also collect and reuse your unwanted plastic bags.

CEREAL OFFENDERS Breakfast cereals are often advertised as a healthy start to the day, but *Which?* magazine found that in many cases this couldn't be further from the truth. *Which?* tested 275 popular cereals and found that you could be breakfasting on as much sugar or salt as you would find in a chocolate bar or a packet of crisps. *Which?* found that 76% of the cereals had a high sugar content, and most of those that didn't were varieties of porridge or shredded wheat. In a separate report, Friends of the Earth found that when tested, 29% of cereals contained pesticide residues. And then there is the infamously wasteful packaging cereals are sold in, with large boxes only half full (in some cases only 40% full). So, for an eco-cereal, pick something organic, with a low sugar, salt and fat content, and which comes in a box or bag roughly the right size for the contents.

USE THE MILKMAN If you buy milk from the supermarket it is likely to come in a non-biodegradable plastic bottle. If you have to make a special trip in your car because you've run out, it can be even more environmentally costly. However, a greener alternative has been quietly working away under our noses for decades. The milkman is virtually an eco-warrior, driving around in his electric vehicle, delivering organic milk to your door in reusable glass bottles. Unfortunately, today milkmen only operate in certain areas. To find out if there is one in your neighbourhood, look on **www.milkdeliveries.co.uk**.

GET YOUR MILK IN A BIODEGRADABLE BOTTLE Most of the milk sold in the UK comes in a plastic bottle. We use nine billion plastic bottles each year, of which only 7% get recycled. The rest go into landfill sites where they can remain for hundreds of years. Instead of adding to this huge pile of plastic, buy your milk in a biodegradable bottle. The Green Bottle (**www.greenbottle.com**) is made mainly of cardboard which can be recycled, or if not it will compost in landfill.

GET YOUR MILK IN AN ECO PAK Calon Wen organic dairy cooperative in Wales has devised a milk pack that uses 75% less plastic than a normal milk bottle. When you buy your first one you also get a jug, which you refill each time you open a new pack of milk, to facilitate storing and pouring. At the time of writing, the Eco Pak, as it's called, was only available at Waitrose stores in Wales, Bath and London, but visit **www. calonwen-cymru.com/eco-pak** to see if it has reached your area yet.

MILK IN A CARTON At least a plastic bottle can be easily recycled. The cartons that milk sometimes comes in are made up of 75% paper, 20% polyethylene and 5% aluminium foil, and are more difficult to recycle, which means they are more likely to end up incinerated or on a landfill site – both environmentally damaging outcomes. However, more and more local councils are now beginning to accept cartons as part of their recycling schemes. To find out if yours does, visit **www.tetrapakrecycling.co.uk**.

TOP TIP – ECOTOPIA.CO.UK
USE AN ECO KETTLE FOR MAKING TEA
Until now, accurately measuring the amount of water to be boiled in your kettle has been a tricky task. The result? It is estimated that, on average, we boil twice the volume of water we need every time. Which means using twice as much energy. An Eco Kettle, however, has an internal reservoir that holds a full capacity of water ready for use, while the measuring button allows any chosen quantity – from a cupful to a pot full – to be released into the separate chamber for boiling. The result? Exactly the right amount of water every time – and no more waste. If everyone boiled only the water they needed to make a cup of tea, instead of filling the kettle each time, we could collectively save enough electricity to run practically all the street lighting in the UK.

AVOID A TEFLON FRY-UP Until about 20 years ago, miners took canaries down into the mines to detect poisonous gases. Canaries are

particularly sensitive to toxic gases, so if they died the miners knew
they had to get out quick. Recently, however, canaries have been dying
in our kitchens. WWF and others blame this on fumes given off by
non-stick Teflon frying pans. Although its findings are disputed by the
chemicals industry, WWF says it has found the perfluorinated compounds
used to make non-stick pans in many different wild animal species,
including polar bears – suggesting the chemicals can travel great distances.
On top of all this, these chemicals are classified as cancer-causing by
the US Environmental Protection Agency and they have been linked
to birth defects. So, heed the warning of the canaries and try frying
your egg in a pan made from some other material, such as cast iron or
stainless steel.

FOLLOW GOOD DISHWASHER PRACTICE Used carefully,
using a dishwasher can be as energy efficient as washing dishes by hand,
according to a study by the University of Bonn. However, the less-quoted
caveat is the fact that, used carelessly, a dishwasher can be much more
wasteful. So, what is good dishwasher practice? Firstly, don't use it just for
the breakfast dishes. It will use the same amount of energy regardless of
what you put in it, so only turn it on when it is full. Rinse plates and scrape
pots to cut out the pre-wash cycle, and open the door to air-dry everything
rather than use the drying part of your machine's cycle. The most
damaging part of a dishwasher is probably the petrochemical detergent
tablet and rinse-aid you use. Instead, use phosphate-free and chlorine-free
tablets and rinse-aid, such as those made by Ecover (**www.ecover.com**).

USE GRANNY'S CLEANERS Long before
supermarket shelves were lined with rows and rows
of toxic cleaning products in brightly coloured
plastic bottles, people kept their houses
spic and span with a few cloths,
some lemon juice, some vinegar
and some bicarbonate of soda.
These traditional techniques, which
were probably used by your granny,

have been revived by Kim and Aggie in the Channel 4 television series *How Clean Is Your House?* The pair have shown that it is possible to clean even the most unbelievably dirty homes with natural products. For lots of cleaning tips visit **www.lowimpact.org**, or ask your granny.

The bathroom routine

COME CLEAN WITH NATURAL SOAP **Soap is the bedrock of the bathroom routine. Yet most commercial soaps are full of polluting chemicals that get washed straight into the water system. Instead, choose from the various brands of natural, organic soap available in health food shops and in natural beauty shops such as Lush (www.lush.co.uk) and The Body Shop (www.thebodyshop.co.uk).**

BAR THE BOTTLE Avoid unnecessary packaging by buying your soap in a bar and not a bottle. It may leave a little soap mark on your sink, but it saves a lot of plastic.

DON'T LEAVE THE TAP RUNNING WHILE YOU BRUSH YOUR TEETH I know, we've all heard this one, but it is worth repeating. If you brush your teeth for the recommended three minutes, and you leave the tap on while you do it, you will waste up to 4.5 litres of water. If you do that twice a day, every day, in one year you will have needlessly used up over 3,000 litres of water. All that water requires energy to clean it and deliver it to your tap, and more energy to reprocess it after it disappears down the drain. So, turn off that tap, it's really not that hard.

TOXIC TOOTHPASTE Of all the products full of chemicals that fill bathroom cabinets up and down the country, possibly the one we should be most concerned about is our toothpaste, as we put it in our mouths. Many commercial toothpastes contain polishing agents and whitening chemicals, such as sodium lauryl sulphate, which can irritate skin and cause ulcers, or triclosan, which is listed as a pesticide in the US. For a more natural alternative, try Tom's of Maine (**www.tomsofmaine.com**), Kingfisher (**www.kingfishertoothpaste.com**) or Green People (**www.greenpeople.co.uk**) toothpaste.

TAKE A SHOWER The average bath uses 80 litres of water, while the average shower uses about half that. A shower is also quicker, giving you a few extra precious minutes in bed. So, if you have the choice, use the shower. And if your house only has a bath, consider putting in a shower – having 40 litres less water to heat each time you wash will soon save you back the money you spend installing it. None of this, incidentally, applies to power showers, which can easily use more water than a bath.

REDUCE YOUR FLUSH Conserving water is primarily important not because we are about to run out, but because of the vast amount of energy used to move it around and clean it. So every time you flush your toilet and eight litres of water gushes down through your pipes, it sets off an energy-intensive chain of events. There are many ways to reduce the amount of water your toilet uses to flush, most of which involve putting objects into the cistern to displace some of the water. These range from a brick to a purpose-made hippo water saver (**www. hippo-the-watersaver.co.uk**). However, the efficiency of these devices will depend on your cistern. An old-fashioned toilet may have a 13-litre flush, in which case reducing this is definitely recommended. Some newer loos, however, have only six-litre flushes, and so you may find the flush just doesn't work properly if you try to reduce it further. The result may be that you have to flush twice each time, causing even more water to be used. The best thing to do is to experiment until you find the right balance.

IF IT'S YELLOW, LET IT MELLOW At the risk of provoking the wrath of tabloid newspaper journalists, as London mayor Ken Livingstone did when he made this very same recommendation, cut down on your flushing altogether by leaving it be if it's only a wee. As the saying goes, 'if it's yellow, let it mellow, if it's brown, flush it down'.

GET A MOONCUP Everyone knows the problems caused by disposable nappies, but disposable sanitary towels also have a huge environmental impact. While you can buy reusable sanitary towels, a Mooncup (**www.mooncup.co.uk**) is a simpler, less messy solution. Instead of absorbing menstrual fluid, it collects it in a silicone cup so you can pour it away. You then rinse the cup and reuse it. The cup, which lasts a few years, can be properly cleaned by placing it in a pan of boiling water for five minutes.

BIODEGRADABLE AND UNBLEACHED If a reusable sanitary towel or a Mooncup is just too weird for you, at the very least use biodegradable and unbleached sanitary towels. Boots the Chemist offers a line of sanitary products that biodegrade within a month. Bleached disposable pads and tampons, meanwhile, can cause health risks as well as environmental damage. A woman can use up to 11,000 tampons in her lifetime, increasing exposure to dioxin, a chemical by-product of bleaching that has been linked to cancers and immune system depression. Tampons also have additives to increase the absorbency, such as surfactants, which can also pose health risks. Added to all of this is the danger of toxic shock syndrome, a rare but potentially very serious illness that has been linked to tampon use. The best advice is to use unbleached organic products.

DON'T FLUSH THEM AWAY Whatever sanitary products you opt for, don't flush them down the loo. Every day in the UK, 2.5 million tampons, 1.4 million sanitary towels and 700,000 panty liners are flushed down the toilet. Almost 70% of all blockages in the sewerage system are attributed to 'disposable' sanitary items, while a great proportion of sanitary waste ends up on our beaches and riverbanks, spoiling our natural environment and creating a potential health risk to humans and wildlife alike.

DON'T USE DISPOSABLE RAZORS It may not be your style, but growing a beard is very eco-friendly. As are hairy legs. Every day, Bic sells around 10 million disposable plastic razors, all of which end up not biodegrading on a landfill site. If you're going for smooth skin, at least avoid all that production and disposal waste by using a reusable razor. And when you are shaving, avoid foams, gels and depilatory creams that contain alkylphenols and potassium thioglycolate. The former is a hormone disrupter, while the latter is a derivative of thioglycolic acid, a highly toxic substance.

Sweet smelling

AU NATURAL **An extravagant bottle of perfume can contain up to 600 synthetic chemicals, most of them made from petroleum and many designated hazardous. There are many natural alternatives that are kinder to the environment and kinder to your skin, such as natural perfumes, essential oils, plant extracts and aromatherapy oils. Culpeper (www.culpeper.co.uk) has a good selection to get you started.**

AVOID PHTHALATES, IF YOU CAN Phthalates are commonly known by environmentalists as 'gender bender' chemicals and can be found in hairspray, perfume, deodorants and nail varnish, as well as in plastic toys, vinyl flooring and car interiors. The omnipresence of phthalates means avoiding them completely is virtually impossible, but you should avoid using them on your body, if possible. Unfortunately, manufacturers are not legally obliged to disclose phthalates on a product's label, and they are often simply labelled as 'fragrance' or with some complicated chemical acronym. To help you decipher cryptic labels in the search for phthalates, visit **www.pollutioninpeople.org/toxics/labels**.

AVOID ARTIFICIAL MUSKS Artificial musks build up in your body and in the environment and can cause headaches, rashes and respiratory problems. Some are also hormone disrupters. Unfortunately, like phthalates, artificial musks don't need to be listed on a product's ingredients, so avoiding them can be difficult. Friends of the Earth campaigns for them to be banned and is also against natural musks, which are extracted from dead musk deer. The only real way to avoid artificial musks is to buy unfragranced products or those scented with essential oils or natural plant ingredients.

AVOID OVER-PACKAGING The late Anita Roddick began offering perfumes, shampoos and moisturisers in refillable bottles as far back as 1976, but few mainstream cosmetics companies have followed The Body Shop's lead. Over 22% of the total product cost of perfumes and cosmetics comes from the packaging as each company tries to outdo the other in convincing you how lavish and luxurious its products are. Don't be fooled by the wasteful packaging – it doesn't make the perfume smell any sweeter. Shun heavily packaged items and if you do have to buy them, leave the box at the shop till and write to the company asking it to set up a refill scheme.

DIY BEAUTY One sure-fire way to cut down on packaging is to make your own beauty products. This may sound daunting, but it is easier than you think. The book *Recipes for Natural Beauty* by Neal's Yard Remedies (**www.nealsyardremedies.com**) will take you through the process, with step-by-step instructions on making chemical-free shampoos, hair dyes, cleansers, moisturisers, toothpastes, hand and nail creams and perfumes. For a free, online DIY make-up guide, visit **www.makeyourowncosmetics.com**.

LOOK GOOD WITHOUT HURTING ANIMALS Every 12 seconds an animal is said to die in a laboratory in the UK. As well as the millions of animals used for medical research, hundreds of thousands more are subjected to painful experiments as part of the development of cosmetics and household goods such as washing up liquid and shoe polish. Buying a product that says 'not tested on animals' is not always a guarantee that no animals have been tested on to produce it, however, as this may only relate to the finished product and not the ingredients. The best guarantee that no animal has been harmed is to buy a product sporting the internationally recognised Go Cruelty Free 'rabbit and stars' logo. For up-to-date information about which companies don't test their

products on animals, visit the Go Cruelty Free website at
www.gocrueltyfree.org.

AVOID AN UNDERARM ASSAULT Even without the now
banned, ozone-depleting CFCs, aerosol antiperspirants are an
environmentally damaging concoction. Many use hydrocarbon
propellants that contribute to air pollution and are thought to be
responsible for respiratory problems. Even if you avoid spraying the
air with chemicals by using a roll-on deodorant, the array of chemicals
it is likely to contain can cause skin and other health problems. Most
antiperspirants, for example, contain aluminium which, when absorbed
through the skin, can cause blood poisoning and has even been linked
with breast cancer. The best option is to go for one of the many 'natural'
roll-on deodorants, such as Aloe Vera deodorant from Green People
(**www.greenpeople.co.uk**), or a deodorant stone made from natural
mineral salts (**www.deodorant-stone.co.uk**).

GET AN AMAZING BODY (STICK) Avoid nasty chemicals
and at the same time cut down on waste by using a Body Stick
(**www.naturalcollection.com**) instead of deodorant. The stick has a
high-grade stainless steel disk at one end that you rub under your arm
for 20 to 30 seconds (which, yes, is quite a long time) to 'neutralise' any
bad odours. The disk never wears out so, in theory, one stick should
last you a lifetime. It is also a good option for people with allergies to
synthetic fragrances and perfumes.

USE ORGANIC COTTON BUDS Cotton buds are eternally
popular, but disposing of them can be problematic because of
the non-biodegradable plastic shaft. Organic cotton buds (from
www.ecotopia.co.uk), have a paper shaft and so break down quicker.
And because they are organic, the cotton farmers use natural methods
instead of toxic chemicals to control pests, such as planting sunflowers
beside the cotton crop to attract pest-eating ants.

Suit care

GREEN IS THE NEW BLACK **In 2006, the UK clothing and textiles industry produced up to two million tonnes of waste, 3.1 million tonnes of CO_2 and 70 million tonnes of waste water. Add to this the fact that many of our clothes are made by poorly paid workers working in appalling conditions in the developing world, and you begin to question whether that £15 shirt really was such a bargain after all. By buying Fairtrade or locally produced organic clothing you really can make a big difference.**

PICK COTTON CAREFULLY Cotton may seem like a gentle, harmless substance, but it is actually hugely problematic. Cotton accounts for 16% of global pesticide use, more than any other single crop. Given that three million people suffer pesticide poisoning each year, resulting in 20,000 deaths – mainly in developing countries where 99% of the world's cotton is grown – the dangers begin to become apparent. One solution that producers have turned to is genetically modified (GM) cotton, which accounts for over 30% of the world's cotton. But the effects of this are unclear, with some scientists predicting catastrophic consequences. Some countries, such as Zambia, are attempting to resist turning to GM cotton against pressure from the pro-GM lobby, preferring instead to turn to organic methods. But with the soils already damaged from conventional cotton growing and the increasing problems being brought about by climate change, it is a tough road to go down. By buying organic cotton, you'll be supporting the brave stance taken by countries like Zambia. With enough demand for their cotton, they may just manage to make it work.

RECYCLE YOUR OLD CLOTHES We all know we should recycle our newspapers and glass bottles, but clothes, too, can be recycled. One and a half billion gallons of oil are used to manufacture the million tonnes of textiles thrown away in the UK each year. Instead of adding to this giant pile of landfill, recycle your unwanted garments. Even if you don't think your local charity shop will be able to sell them, the fibres from most clothes can be shredded and rewoven to make new clothes, or industrial rags at worst. Some charity shops will take clothes and recycle them in this way regardless of their condition. If your local shop doesn't want your old suits and ties, put them in a clothes bank (like a bottle bank, but for recycling clothes), or ask your local council if it takes them as part of its door-to-door recycling service.

SECOND-HAND CLOTHES Buying second-hand clothes cuts out all the waste and transport emissions generated by producing new items of clothing, as well as cutting down on landfill. You may have to rummage through lots of 1970s suits in musty second-hand shops, but there are bargains to be had for the persistent. If that's not for you, perhaps you could hold a swap shop with your friends to freshen up your wardrobe.

TURN YOUR WASHING MACHINE DOWN You probably don't need me to tell you this one, after all the noise being made by companies such as M&S and Ariel – including expensive television adverts featuring supermodels. The ads tell us that it's OK to use their products as long as we wash our clothes at 30ºC. Well, despite the cynicism of environmentalists who question the motives of these big firms, it is a good idea for most washes as it uses a third less energy when compared to washing at 60ºC.

GREEN WASH What Ariel and co don't mention, however, is the environmental damage done by using their detergents, which send a brew of harmful chemicals out into the water system. Instead, use an eco-friendly product such as Simply (**www.simplywashing.com**), which is the first UK laundry powder to be awarded the EU Eco-label.

NUTS TO SOAP POWDERS Cut out washing powders altogether by putting some Eco-balls in your washing machine (**www.ecoballsdirect.co.uk**), which produce ionised oxygen to naturally activate water molecules, allowing them to penetrate into clothing fibres and lift dirt away. The balls, which have had mixed reviews, can be used up to 1,000 times and cost, on average, 3p a wash. As there is no detergent, the machine's rinse cycle can be reduced, saving on electricity. They are also hypoallergenic, so they are good for people with sensitive skin, including babies and children. Another solution is organic Soapods, or soap nuts, (**www.soapods.com**) which grow on soapnut trees in India and Nepal – so they are an entirely renewable source. Soap nuts contain an active, natural ingredient similar to soap, which is released when the nuts come into contact with water.

DON'T USE THE DRYER Try to organise your washing schedule so you don't need to use the dryer – ie don't leave it until Sunday night. Tumble dryers are the most energy-consuming appliances we use in the home. If you do buy one, gas appliances may be more expensive, but they cost half as much to run and produce 33% less greenhouse emissions.

USE AN ECO WASHING LINE Of course, we don't all have nice big gardens with washing lines to hang our clothes out in. And, anyway, often it is raining. Eco Washing Lines has obviously heard all these excuses before and has assembled a huge range of indoor drying options to fit any nook or cranny your house may offer, from wall-mounted dryers to balcony dryers. Or, for something a little more traditional, why not install a Gnu clothes airer over the stove in your kitchen (high ceilings required!)? Visit **www.ecowashinglines.co.uk**.

LEAST-CONSUMING DRYER If you decide you simply have to have a tumble dryer, use the website **www.sust-it.net** to find out which model uses the least energy. The site tells you how much energy each popular model uses for each wash and it works out how much this is likely to cost you depending on your electricity supplier. As well as tumble dryers, the site gives the same information for all the other white goods, as well as popular entertainment devices (TVs, DVD players etc).

DRY-CLEANERS A biodynamic wine stain on your suit? The only thing for it is a trip to the dry-cleaners. However, most dry-cleaners primarily use a substance called perchloroethylene (PERC), which has been linked to numerous health problems in dry-cleaning workers and even in people who live nearby. Its use is highly controlled, but if it does escape into the atmosphere or the water system it can cause significant environmental damage. Many 'dry-clean only' garments can, with care, be wet cleaned, but a better alternative is to dry-clean them using a newly developed silicone-based substance called GreenEarth®. This is non-toxic, carries no health warnings and quickly degrades into sand if spilt. To find a dry-cleaner in your area using this substance rather than PERC, visit **www.greenearth.co.uk**.

ECO-SHOES (WHATEVER NEXT!) We don't often think about what our shoes are made from, but if it's not a dead animal, then it's probably some environmentally problematic material, such as polyurethane, nylon or PVC. Instead, get yourself some smart, leather-free, environmentally friendly shoes – they do exist. Visit **www.greenshoes. co.uk** or **www.vegetarian-shoes.co.uk**.

The commute

According to a recent study, UK workers spend an average of 92 minutes a day travelling to and from work. Most of that travel time takes place in cars. Although the proportion of people driving to work fell from 92% in 2003/4 to 75% in 2005/6, suggesting the green message is getting through, that's still a lot of people on the roads. Private cars produce 10% of the UK's total CO_2 emissions, so reducing the number of drivers further could make a big difference. As well as being less polluting, other forms of transport can be quicker and cheaper, particularly if you live in a city. Yet, according to the figures, only 3% of people walk to work, 2% cycle and just 1% catch the bus. So, make a difference by getting out of your car and trying an alternative form of transport, such as the train or the bus, cycling or walking. And even if you do drive, think about what you drive and how you drive it, as that, too, can affect the amount of pollution you create.

Green driving

LEARN TO DRIVE PROPERLY The majority of us drive to work and probably still will even after reading this book. But if you do, there are still things you can do to reduce fuel consumption, and hence reduce your environmental impact. An advanced driving course (www.bsm.co.uk) will teach you about safety and efficiency. You'll learn, for example, that pulling away too quickly uses up to 60% more fuel, while changing gear at the right time can reduce fuel usage by 15%. Taking an advanced course will also significantly reduce your car insurance, and there is a special Pass Plus course (www.passplus.org.uk) for people who have just passed their test.

LOSE SOME BAGGAGE To be greener, take any unnecessary weight off your car. Remove any bulky items you don't need from the boot, such as buggies, tools or golf clubs. The lighter your car, the less your engine will have to work and the less fuel it will burn.

DON'T GET DRAGGED DOWN Drag will also make your engine work harder, so conserve fuel by keeping windows and sunroofs closed, when possible. A roof rack will also cause drag, so remove it if you have one you're not using.

CHECK YOUR TYRE PRESSURE Another simple thing you can do to improve the efficiency of your car is to check the tyre pressure. Every 6psi – the measure for pressure – that your tyre is under-inflated will increase your fuel consumption by 1%. So take a moment to top up with air, which is free at most garages, and you'll be able to spend less topping up with expensive and polluting petrol.

DON'T BE A BOY RACER When driving, avoid accelerating or braking too quickly. By driving safely and sensibly and keeping your distance from the vehicles in front, you can improve your fuel efficiency. And don't drive too fast. Not only is it dangerous, but the faster you drive above 60mph, the more fuel you use and the more pollution you cause.

KEEP UP Having said that driving too fast burns up more fuel, it should also be pointed out that driving too slow is not good either. In fact, travelling at less than 15mph creates the most pollution. Because of this, traffic jams are bad news in every way. If your work allows you to commute outside of rush hour, not only will you waste less time stuck in a queue, but you'll waste less fuel, too. If a jam gets really bad, or you find yourself sitting in your car not moving at any other time, turn your engine off, as leaving it to idle will waste fuel. In Toronto, Canada, you can be fined up to $5,000 if you leave your engine idling for more than three minutes. In fact, idling for anything longer than 10 seconds will use more fuel than restarting your engine.

TURN DOWN THE AIR CON If your car has air conditioning, only use it when you really need it. Air conditioning relies on your engine working harder to support it, which increases fuel consumption. Use air vents to cool the car as much as possible, as opening windows will create drag.

FUEL CHOICES The type of fuel you choose will affect the amount and type of emissions your car gives off. It is estimated that 24,000 people die prematurely in the UK each year as a result of vehicle pollution, so the choice you make is quite literally a matter of life and death. The two options most people consider are petrol and diesel. Diesel cars are usually named as the more environmentally friendly of the two because they use fuel more efficiently. However, while diesel may produce less CO_2, which causes global warming, it also produces higher levels of certain other pollutants, such as nitrogen oxides.

HYBRID One alternative is to go for a hybrid car, such as the Toyota Prius, which uses less fuel because it has an electric motor that helps the engine when accelerating. The electric motor then recharges itself while the car is driving at a constant speed.

GO ELECTRIC Electric cars produce no CO_2 or other polluting exhaust emissions and are very cheap to run. However, with top speeds of under 60mph and a range of less than 100 miles, they are really only useful if you live in a city, where you travel shorter distances at slower speeds. Aside from the popular G-Wiz car (**www.goingreen.co.uk**), Alternative Vehicles Technology (**www.avt.uk.com**) sells a number of small cars converted to run on electricity. And if you fancy something on two wheels, the Vectrix scooter (**www.vectrix.co.uk**) has an impressive top speed of 62mph.

GAS Many petrol and diesel engines can be converted to run on liquefied petroleum gas (LPG), which produces fewer emissions of carbon dioxide, hydrocarbons, carbon monoxide and nitrous oxides than both petrol and diesel, and is much cheaper. According to The Green Fuel Company (**www.greenfuel.org.uk**) the 100,000 LPG vehicles currently driving on Britain's roads represent a saving of around 80,000 tonnes of CO_2 per annum compared with petrol, and substantial local air quality benefits compared with diesel. To find out about how to convert your car to gas, visit **www.envirogas.co.uk** or **www.gascarco.com**.

OTHER FUELS Most other alternative fuel options are still in their infancy, at least in the UK. Hydrogen, for example, is a naturally occurring element that emits just water and air when it is used as fuel. It is, however, virtually impossible to find somewhere to fill up your hydrogen car in the UK. There are a few buses in London running on hydrogen, but this is more of a showcase example than a genuine alternative, at least for now.

WHAT'S WRONG WITH BIOFUEL? Bio-diesel, another alternative fuel, has been causing heated debate among environmentalists for some time. It is produced from renewable sources such as sugar beet, rape seed, palm oil and sunflowers, and it is carbon-neutral – this is because the carbon dioxide produced when it is burned is the same as the carbon dioxide absorbed from the atmosphere by the plants used to make it. It sounds like the perfect green fuel. However, the fact that vast amounts of rainforest and arable land are being cleared to grow the raw materials is leading to environmental problems and food shortages in some parts of the world. Campaigners say these shortages will get much worse if biofuel catches on in a big way. Although production of the fuel is still relatively small-scale, the first signs of problems are already apparent, with many experts linking tortilla riots in Mexico, where the price of maize rose by 400%, and pasta protests in Italy over the rising price of pasta, to the increased production of biofuel.

MAKE YOUR OWN BIOFUEL If you are particularly enterprising, you can create your own biofuel by collecting old oil from restaurants or chip shops and filtering it yourself – an eco-solution that won't lead to food shortages. Biofuel will only work in a converted diesel engine. To learn how to convert your car and make your own fuel, you could take a course at either the Low Impact Living Initiative (**www.lowimpact.org**) or the Centre for Alternative Technology (**www.cat.org.uk**). If you want to buy ready-made biofuel made from recycled oil, you will have to find a local supplier, such as Sundance Renewables (**www.sundancerenewables. org.uk**) in Wales.

EFFICIENCY Whatever fuel type you opt for, choosing a fuel-efficient car will reduce your emissions. Generally, a car with a smaller engine will use less fuel for the same journey. The government recently launched a website (**www.dft.gov.uk/ActOnCO2**) in connection with *What Car?* magazine to inform buyers of the greenest models in each class of vehicle, so if you really need a larger car, you can still choose the greenest model available. Even those vilified 4x4s have varying shades of green. At the time of writing, the least polluting large 4x4, for example, with its 2.2-litre diesel engine, was the Hyundai New Santa Fe.

FIT A FUEL SAVER DEVICE Fitting a fuel-saving device into the fuel line that feeds your engine can reduce your car's harmful emissions by up to 40% and save you up to 10% on fuel costs. Although the improvements are more dramatic on older cars, the devices will make a difference to petrol, diesel or gas-powered vehicles. To find out more visit **www.powerplus.be** or **www.ecotekplc.com**.

DON'T DRIVE SHORT DISTANCES If you live within two miles of your workplace, there is yet another reason not to take the car. Besides the fact that you live within easy walking or cycling distance, the catalytic converter, which helps cut down your car's carbon monoxide emissions, does not become effective until after the first two miles, making shorter distances even more polluting.

CAR WASH If you are a car owner you probably clean your vehicle once in a while. If you are really proud of your car you may wash it more frequently. Depending on how you do it and how careful you are, washing a car can use up a lot of water. Professional washes can use over a hundred litres at a time. Some may be more efficient, such as the award-winning Pit Stop car washing service in Swansea, which uses a water recycling system to reduce its water consumption by 60%. Ask your local washers what they are doing to be more efficient, and if they look at you like you're mad, try somewhere else. If you wash your car at home with a bucket of water rather than a hose, you can keep your water usage down to just a few litres. However, if you do, avoid washing it in the street, as the soapy run-off will enter the storm drains and feed directly into rivers. Instead, wash your car on gravel or grass.

WASH WITHOUT WATER If you are particularly concerned about the amount of water needed to clean your car, take it to a waterless car washing service such as Aqua Nought (**www.aquanought.co.uk**). Instead of water, they use a fine, biodegradable spray, which is then rubbed off with a cloth. To go waterless at home, buy your own biodegradable, non-toxic magic spray from Eco Touch (**www.ecotouch.net**).

RECYCLE YOUR CAR You may only drive new cars, part exchanging them with a dealer once they get a few years old. But eventually all cars come to the end of their useful life and if you are in possession of one you will probably wonder what to do with it. In 2005 the government passed legislation to ensure that all no-longer-wanted cars (End of Life Vehicles, it calls them) are recycled, so all you have to do is find your nearest Authorised Treatment Facility. To do this, visit **www.recycleyourcar.co.uk**.

Other ways to go

TAKE PUBLIC TRANSPORT **Traffic congestion makes a lot of people late for work and costs the country around £15 billion each year. A double-decker bus, however, can carry the same number of people as 40 half-occupied cars, yet takes up just a fraction of the road space. Driving a car to work is also less fuel efficient, and hence more polluting. One litre of fuel can carry a person four miles in a large car, 31 miles in a bus with 40 passengers and 34 miles in a train with 300 passengers.**

PEDAL POWER Cycling is one of the most highly recommended forms of green commuter transport. It is noise free, congestion free, emissions free (apart from those generated in the bike's production), it is cheap and, if you live in a large city, it is probably the quickest way to get to work. As well as being good for the planet, cycling is also good for your health. According to a study of 10,000 civil servants, those who cycle at least 20 miles a week (the equivalent of a two-mile daily commute) are half as likely to suffer heart disease.

DOWN BY THE RIVER Make your daily cycle more pleasant by finding a traffic-free route. The National Cycle Network provides over 10,000 miles of walking and cycle routes on traffic-free paths, quiet lanes and traffic-calmed roads around the UK. For details and a map of the routes, visit **www.sustrans.org.uk**. Another traffic-free option is to use canal towpaths. For route suggestions and details of the Towpath Code of Conduct, visit **www.waterscape.com**.

CASE STUDY
ANDREW STEVENSON FROM MANCHESTER

Andrew cycles 10 miles each way to work at Aquinas Sixth Form College in Stockport and found that quite a few teachers and staff were approaching him and other cyclists to ask about good routes. 'I found myself regularly taping together photocopied pages of the A to Z to show people my route (which I'm really proud of as it crosses five parks and avoids main roads),' he says, 'and others were doing the same.' So, together with a colleague, he decided to set up a forum where people could publicise their routes, as well as discuss other cycling issues. The response was very positive and they even managed to persuade the college to increase covered bike racks and fit a shower for cyclists. They also arrange a regular visit from their local bike shop repairman, who sets up in the car park once a term. They now run a regular newsletter, called the Bicycle Courier, which all staff receive electronically via the college intranet, so no paper is involved. 'Quite a few people who live too far away to cycle have even told me that they've started cycling more at weekends,' says Andrew.

GET A FOLD-UP BIKE Despite the multitude of benefits cycling brings, there are many excuses for not using one to get to work. Some of these are resolved by buying a folding bike. This can easily be taken on trains, the London Underground and even on buses, if you need to combine different types of transport on your commute. It will also fit easily in the back of a car or a taxi. And if you're worried about your bike being stolen, you can usually bring a folded bike into the office with you and store it under your desk rather than leave it out on the street. There are lots of different types of folding bike on the market, such as the Brompton (**www.bromptonbicycle.co.uk**), the Strida (**www.strida.co.uk**) and Sir Clive Sinclair's latest invention, the A-bike (**www.a-bike.co.uk**).

CASE STUDY
AOIFE GALLAGHER FROM DUBLIN

Aoife loves talking about her daily commute. After moving from the city centre out to the suburbs, her daily commute went from a 20-minute bike ride to a 90-minute slog combining a bus, a jammed train and a long walk. 'In an effort to be greener, and stay reasonably fit, I tried biking some of it. I tried cycling to the train on my husband's bike, which I left at the station, taking the train and then getting on my own bike and cycling to work. The problem was that our bikes were in constant danger of being nicked from the station bike rails, and also there was no flexibility – I couldn't get a lift home or take a taxi or a bus, as that would mean abandoning my bike. Plus, at the weekend, I couldn't use my bike to go shopping or anything. So, I got a folding bike. Now my bike is always with me, on the train, on the bus, in the taxi or car, in the pub, in restaurants, in the park etc. It has saved me a lot of hassle. I used to leave at 7.30am, and get to work at 9am, if I was lucky. Now I leave my house at 8.15am and always get to work before 9am.'

GET AN ELECTRIC BIKE If cycling is just too energetic for you (perhaps you live in a very hilly area, you have an injury or you're just too lazy), then you could consider an electric bike. Although not as eco-friendly as a normal bicycle, it is nevertheless a very green mode of transport. You have the option to use the pedal power, the electric motor or a combination of the two, depending on the terrain, slope or just how tired you are. Other advantages over a conventional bike are speed and the fact that you don't have to arrive at work dripping with sweat.

RECYCLE YOUR BICYCLE If you decide to invest in a new bike, don't just bin your old one, recycle it. You could try selling it on eBay or in the local paper. Even if you think it is beyond repair, a bike recycling project such as the Bike Station (**www.thebikestation.org.uk**) in Edinburgh will find some use for the parts. Alternatively, donate your old bike to the charity ReCycle, which ships unwanted bicycles to people in Africa, who use them for collecting water or riding to work or school. Visit **www.re-cycle.org**.

SIGN UP TO A RESCUE SERVICE If you've decided to try cycling but are a fair-weather cyclist, worrying about how to get home if it starts pouring with rain, then fear no more. If you live in London, the taxi firm

Climate Cars (**www.climatecars.com**) runs a bike rescue service to take you and your bike home. This may also prove useful if you head out for a drink and have one too many. And although it's quite costly, the money you save from cycling will pay for an occasional call-out.

BRING THE KIDS   Need to drop your kids off at school or playgroup on the way to work? Well, that doesn't mean you can't cycle. Even if you have more than one kid to transport, there are still ways and means. A bike trailer (**www.bikesandtrailers.com**) will hold two children, as will the stylish Kangaroo bike (**www.kangaroobike.com**), or the traditional Christiania bike (**www.christianiabikes.com**).

ECO-LIGHTS   We talk about the environmental problems associated with batteries in chapter 8, but you can avoid these issues, and the cost of forever having to buy new batteries, by investing in some dynamo lights. Dynamo lights have been around for decades and are powered by the motion of your bicycle. For frictionless dynamo lights that won't slow your bike down, visit **www.freelights.co.uk**.

TOP TIP – SUSTRANS
CARBON-FREE COMMUTING!

Get on your bike for a leaner and greener commute! Cycling is often the quickest way to get around town and it's the least polluting, after walking. It helps keep you fit, healthy and young – regular cyclists enjoy fitness levels of someone 10 years their junior – and, once you've bought your bike, running costs are next to nothing. Wear trainers when you pedal and take your office shoes in your bag, and ladies you can wear skirts when cycling, just slip a pair of shorts on underneath and change when you get into work. Keep a spare top and pair of socks in your desk drawer in case you get caught in a downpour – but, surprisingly, in the UK it only rains hard on about eight working days a year. So what's your excuse for not trying two wheels for your commute? For information on commuting by bike and to find a cycle route near you, visit **www.sustrans.org.uk** or call 0845 113 0065.

WALK TO WORK What, use just my own two legs and nothing else to get to work? For many of us in twenty-first-century Britain it may seem like a preposterous idea, but there is no greener, cheaper or more reliable way to get to work than to walk. It is also great for your health. If you live in London, Birmingham or Edinburgh, you can use **www.walkit.com** to help plan your route.

LIVE NEAR TO WORK Of course, to walk to work you will need to live near to your office. When moving house, factor your commute into the equation when deciding where to live. Consider the financial and environmental costs of having to make a long journey twice a day – as well as the cost in terms of your sanity and the number of waking hours you'll spend in transit. If you can't live near to where you work, try to negotiate some home-working time into your weekly schedule. If everybody worked from home one day a week, there would be 20% fewer commuters clogging up roads and squeezing on to buses and trains every day.

On the road

READ A BOOK **If you spend hours each day sitting on trains or waiting for buses, rather than plug in your laptop, or listen to your iPod, try reading a book instead. This ancient activity requires no further energy than your hand to turn the pages and the materials and energy used in its initial production.**

READ SOMETHING GREEN Read a book about being green. Oh, you already are. Well, once you have finished this one, there are many more books to inspire you to a greener life, from books on cooking seasonal food, to building an eco-house. Visit **www.greenbooks.co.uk**, **www.earthscan.co.uk** or any good bookshop.

SET YOUR BOOK FREE Make better use of resources by sharing your books, particularly ones you like. If you don't have a willing friend

to give it to, set it off on a journey by registering it at the website
www.bookcrossing.com, and then leaving it somewhere conspicuous,
such as on the train. When someone picks it up, they will hopefully
find your note telling them to log on to the Book Crossing website and
to register where the book has ended up. You can then see what has
happened to your book. If the person that finds it reads it and then
passes it on again, your book may end up on a magical journey halfway
across the world.

GREEN METROPOLIS Another way to recycle your old books is
to sell them. The website **www.greenmetropolis.com** will give you £3
for any paperbacks it sells on your behalf. If you want to complete the
recycling circle by buying a second-hand book from Green Metropolis,
they cost £3.75, including delivery. Of course, if you are feeling altruistic,
you could take your books to your local charity shop and let it benefit
from reselling them. Either way, recycling books will help minimise waste
and the energy used to produce new books.

STAY INFORMED Rather than keeping up with celebrity gossip by
reading *Heat* magazine, use your reading time to stay on top of the issues

affecting the planet you live on. Take out a subscription to *The Ecologist* magazine (**www.theecologist.org**), *Resurgence* (**www.resurgence.org**) or *Green Futures* magazine (**www.greenfutures.org.uk**).

DITCH YOUR IPOD FOR A WIND-UP MP3 PLAYER Look

around any given commuter train or bus on any given weekday and it is highly likely that a fair proportion of your fellow passengers will be nodding their heads gently with little white headphones attached to their ears. Podcasts, iPods and MP3 downloads are everywhere but, of course, all of these devices require pre-charging or batteries. Except one. Trevor Baylis, the inventor of the wind-up radio, has now produced a wind-up MP3 player, which is available from all good eco-shops, such as ethicalsuperstore.com. As well as being green, it means your device will never run out of juice, so you can keep on nodding, even after all the Duracell-powered devices have died and their toxic batteries have been thrown on a landfill site somewhere.

TOP TIP – BRIGIT FROM BBC2'S *IT'S NOT EASY BEING GREEN*

TEA ON THE GO

When travelling by British Rail, take your own flask of tea or coffee. This means you avoid being tempted by the onboard hot drinks, which come in paper cups with plastic lids, in a little paper bag, and with little plastic tubs of milk and a wooden stick for stirring, all of which get scooped up at the end of the journey into a black bin liner.

Office hours

Turn your personal space into a shining beacon of
environmentally friendly office space. In most offices, your
desk is largely your own domain and it is here that you have the
most control to effect change. Get a plant. A fountain pen. A
mousemat made from recycled Ribena cartons. And leave out
obvious signs of your greenness, such as a cycle helmet on your
desk or a wind-up radio, so that colleagues become interested.
Your positive example of a green working utopia will be a much
more effective tool for spreading the green word than posting
up messages on the office noticeboard. Before you know it, you
may have inspired your office to go green without having to
tackle the bureaucracy of 'management'. Power to the people,
as Citizen Smith used to say.

Around the office

GIVE YOURSELF A LIFT **Taking the stairs instead of the lift is one of those things we all know we should do, but when we arrive at work after a long commute, the steep winding staircase is often the last thing we feel like tackling. Of course, it depends on how many floors you have to ascend, but the benefits of using the stairs are manifold. Firstly you're using carbon-free leg muscle power instead of large amounts of electricity. Plus, it's an extremely good work-out, burning up flab and toning your leg muscles. You'll also feel good about yourself when you've done it, and you'll have avoided any awkward silent lift encounters.**

LIKE CLOCKWORK Although the wind-up radio was originally invented to help spread Aids awareness to remote parts of Africa, it is also a good way to cut down on your office's energy consumption in a fun way. Radios may use up relatively small amounts of electricity, but you can cut out even that by employing muscle power instead. Most wind-up radios need winding every hour or so, so it gives you an excuse to take a regular screen break from your computer – recommended for good eye health and for the prevention of repetitive strain injury. If you work outdoors, a wind-up radio is even more beneficial as it means you don't need to use environmentally damaging batteries and it will never run out of juice – as long as you have the energy to wind it, that is. Most online eco-stores, such as **www.naturalcollection.com**, sell wind-up radios.

DON'T USE AIR FRESHENERS The phrase 'air freshener' is largely an oxymoron, because most pollute the air, rather than freshen it. Filled with a whole host of chemicals and volatile organic compounds (VOCs), they have been linked with an array of ailments, including headaches, lung damage and even postnatal depression. Instead of filling the air with chemicals, use a natural air freshener from an eco-shop such as www.naturalcollection.com or www.ecotopia.co.uk, or open a window. And whatever you do, avoid plug-in air fresheners, which use electricity to pump the chemicals around the office – it would be hard to come up with a less eco-friendly product.

GET SOME CURTAINS Curtains are not often used in offices, but they are excellent at keeping heat in during the night, meaning less energy is wasted reheating the office each morning. Blinds, more commonly used in offices, are principally designed for keeping sunlight out in the summer rather than for keeping heat in. Make sure your new office curtains fit well and, for maximum effect, get them thermal lined.

OPEN THE BLINDS If it doesn't render your screen invisible, open your curtains or blinds during the day and let the sunlight in. As well as reducing the need for artificial lights, sunlight will heat the office, cutting down on heating costs. Make sure the light is not blocked by the poor positioning of filing cabinets, plants or any other large objects you may have in your workplace.

FLICKERING LIGHTS Report flickering lights to your building's facilities manager – and if you don't have one, change the lights yourself. Faulty lights will not only stress you out and contribute to sick building syndrome (see chapter 14), but they also use up more electricity.

SHUT THE DOOR Keep rooms warm by shutting doors where possible. Draughts will gush in through large openings such as doorways, bringing down room temperatures. The heating will then have to work harder to keep staff from freezing. It works the other way, too, of course. If it's too hot, open the door to let the heat out rather than turning up the air conditioning.

CLIMATE CONTROL Rather than turn the heating or air conditioning up if you are too cold or too hot – or asking the building manager to if you are in a big office – regulate your temperature by putting on more clothes or taking some off, within reason, of course.

If your office is too smart for one of your Christmas jumpers, wear a vest under your shirt instead.

UNPLUG YOUR PHONE CHARGER We have heard this countless times, but we're still not doing it. According to the phone company O_2, only 5% of the energy used by the UK's mobile phone chargers is actually used to charge phones – the rest is used when the charger is left plugged into the wall but not switched off at the socket. That's over 50,000 tonnes of carbon dioxide emissions that would be avoided if we could all just switch off our chargers after use. How hard can it be?

Desk space

SCREEN WIPES Clean your computer screen with an E-Cloth. These cleverly designed cloths cut out the need for harmful chemical sprays and just require a little bit of water to work effectively. E-Cloths can be used on any hard surface, but work best on glass, chrome and stainless steel. Visit www.e-cloth.com.

DESK CLEANING A study from the University of Arizona recently found that the average desk was covered in more germs than a toilet seat. But before you dig out the industrial cleaner, consider a more eco-friendly cleaning option, such as those sold by Ecover (**www.ecover.com**). Even better is to research and try out some of the 'granny's cleaning tips' mentioned in the Monday Morning chapter. Here's one to get you started: To remove watermarks on a wooden surface, such as a desktop, rub half a

brazil nut on to the offending area, making sure the surface is completely dry. Alternatively, try applying a splodge of toothpaste on a damp cloth to the watermark.

GET AN ECO-FRIENDLY DESK LIGHT If you need a bright desk light, try to get one that uses an LED (which stands for light-emitting diode) bulb. These are more energy efficient than standard bulbs and can produce a strong, directed light. And if you have a desk light, and no one else is in the office, turn off the main light. Nigel's Eco Store (**www.nigelsecostore.com**) sells an LED desk light made from black walnut wood grown in sustainably managed forests, which sounds like the perfect eco-solution, although it is quite pricey.

GET A PLANT FOR YOUR DESK Rather than douse the office in a 'faux flower' scented air freshener, get a plant for your desk. Not only will it smell nice, naturally, but it will also absorb all the harmful chemicals given off by your office equipment, carpets and furniture. To find out which plants are best for your office, you could invest in the book *Eco-Friendly Houseplants*, by former NASA scientist Bill Wolverton – available at all good bookshops. For dim offices he recommends the genus *Dracaena* and the common spider plant, among others.

GIVE UP YOUR BIN Having a bin under your desk may be convenient, but this convenience may be making you more wasteful. If you have to get up from your seat to put something in the bin, you are more likely to think of another use for it or, at the very least, walk to the nearest recycling point instead.

TURN YOUR COMPUTER OFF AT NIGHT Leaving your computer on overnight might mean you can restart work fractionally faster the next morning, but at a significant cost to the environment. If a thousand people read this and as a result turn off their computers when they head home each evening, it will save 180 tonnes of CO_2 emissions every year. So, go on, shut it down. And while you're at it, make sure the screen, printer and any other peripherals are off, too.

BUT MY IT DEPARTMENT TELLS ME NOT TO Many large companies run security and software updates during the night and so ask workers to log out but leave their computers switched on when they go home. This, of course, can use up a lot of energy. Instead, suggest running updates at start-up or at some other point during the day. The IT department may be unlikely to change its position without intervention from the board, so if you find it is unwilling to change, try approaching your boss with the suggestion – remembering to mention that it will save the company money.

SCREEN SAVER IS NO PLANET SAVER Screen savers do not save energy. They are primarily intended to prevent screen burn – where an image that has been left unchanged for too long makes a permanent impression on the screen. Instead, change the settings so that your computer switches off automatically if it is left idle for a certain amount of time.

TOP TIP – SELFSUFFICIENTISH.COM
TAX THE SLACK

Does it drive you mad that some people never turn their monitors off when they leave the office, no matter what you do and how many times you tell them? With the help of the others in the office you can overcome this by suggesting a green tax. This has to be paid each time a monitor, photocopier or printer is left on. Charge between 50p and £1 a day and spend the money on cakes for everyone who did turn off their machines. You should hopefully make more friends than enemies doing this. To be even greener, you could donate part of the money to Friends of the Earth or some other environmental charity.

DON'T HOG THE HEAT Don't place your desk right in front of the radiator. It may keep your legs warm, but energy will also be wasted heating your desk – which is unnecessary as desks, as far as we know, don't mind the cold. Stopping heat from reaching the rest of the room will probably result in someone else feeling cold and turning up the heating, burning up more energy.

DON'T SIT TOO CLOSE TO YOUR PRINTER Make sure the printer is situated away from your desk to reduce the chances of being affected by the toxic fumes it gives off (see chapter 8). Keeping the printer at more than arm's length will also give you a reason to get away from your monitor and stretch your legs for a few seconds every now and then.

Stationery cupboard

USE A SOLAR-POWERED CALCULATOR **Long before green was trendy, solar-powered calculators were mainstream. This was a good thing, as batteries are incredibly wasteful – they produce 50 times less energy than it takes to make them. So go old-school and make sure your calculator is powered by the sun.**

CALENDARS, DIARIES AND THINGS Your computer is probably on for most of the working day so, rather than have a paper calendar or diary on your desk, use the ones on your computer. As well as saving on paper, and hence saving energy and trees, online calendars and diaries have other advantages, including electronic reminders so you don't miss meetings.

RECYCLED MOUSE MAT A mouse mat is something that can easily be made from recycled materials. By getting yourself a recycled mouse mat, you're not only saving the energy used to make a new one, but you are encouraging recycling in general by completing the circle – without people buying recycled products, there would be less incentive to produce recycled products and hence less incentive to recycle. Recycled Business Gifts (**www.recycledbusinessgifts.co.uk**) produces custom-made recycled mouse mats from tyres, computer circuit boards, juice cartons and vending machine cups.

OTHER RECYCLED STUFF As well as mouse mats, you can kit your eco-desk out with recycled pens, notebooks, pencils, rulers and the rest. If your stationery is provided for you, why not suggest it to the stationery purchaser? In most cases the cost difference is minimal, but it may help staff feel better about their working environment. For a good selection of recycled office items, visit **www.remarkable.co.uk**.

USE A FOUNTAIN PEN If your office is anything like mine, ballpoint pens regularly grow legs and run away during the night, meaning countless trips to the stationery cupboard to get more. Each of these little implements requires energy to make and transport from factories on the other side of the world. Then, as they are made of non-biodegradable plastic, wherever they end up they will sit for hundreds of years, creating a sea of pen litter for future generations. Instead, invest in a refillable fountain pen and a bottle of ink (not cartridges). The result? Less plastic, nicer writing and your pen is less likely to disappear.

NOTE THIS DOWN ON A SCRAP OF USED PAPER Rather than order tonnes of Post-it® notes and notebooks just for jotting down telephone messages and the like, collect all those print-outs that go wrong or are no longer needed and tear them into smaller pieces of paper for making notes. This is the full recycling circle in action on your desk – saving paper and reducing landfill.

PRINT LESS Think twice before hitting Ctrl + P (the shortcut for sending a file to print). Do you really need to print it? If it is to show other employees or clients, can you email them instead? Things like instructions or training manuals work better online because they can be easily updated if someone spots a mistake or procedures change in any way. With hard copies, updating means another wasteful print run.

ADD TO BOOKMARKS If you find an interesting website while surfing the net but you're worried you might never find it again, rather than print it out, bookmark it (or add it to your 'favourites' depending on your browser's terminology). This should be one of the main options along the top of the browser while you are surfing. If you intend to bookmark lots of pages, organise them into folders using the 'organise bookmarks' option.

GET OTHERS TO PRINT LESS You can quickly and easily add a line to the bottom of every email you send urging your recipients to be green and not print out the email. Write something like: 'Help save waste, don't print this email'. To do this in Outlook Express, click on the Tools menu, then Options and then click on the Signatures tab. Click New, type your message and then click Add. Other email packages should work in a similar way.

DON'T FAX Unless you really think you need one, think twice before buying a fax machine. As well as adding yet another plastic-coated electrical device to the office, it means printing things out on sheets of paper and then copying them onto other sheets of paper on other fax machines in other offices. In most cases, transferring this information can be done much more efficiently using email.

JUNK THE MAIL You may well receive even more junk mail at work than you do at home. Put a stop to it by returning any unwanted mail and marking it 'return to sender' or actively asking to be taken off mailing lists – a quick phone call or email should suffice. When visiting conferences and trade shows, try to give your details only to companies that genuinely interest you. Beware of those boxes that ask you to use your business card to enter a prize draw – they are usually a way to collect contact details so that you can be bombarded with junk mail and spam. And try to recycle any mail you do receive.

COLLECT STAMPS Although most junk mail you receive is unlikely to be stamped, you can collect the stamps from any mail that is and give them to charity. Although it is a bit of a dying practice, there are still many charities that raise funds by selling on used stamps – turning something that would otherwise be binned into cash. The Royal National Institute of Blind People (**www.rnib.org.uk**) is one large charity that still collects stamps, otherwise you could try offering them to your local charity shop, church or youth group.

Take a break

Trying to find a healthy snack in the UK can sometimes be difficult. If you are feeling peckish and you walk into your local shop you will probably find yourself staring at rows and rows of chocolate bars, crisps and sweets. Sometimes it can be hard to turn around and leave without buying anything, so it may not come as a surprise that almost 80% of the crisps eaten in Europe are bought in the UK – that's around six billion bags a year, or a tonne of crisps every three minutes. As well as being unhealthy, virtually all of these crisps come in unrecyclable bags. Even the few healthy snacks you may be able to find are not problem-free. Bananas and apples are probably grown half-way around the world and doused in pesticides, while nuts also come in unrecyclable bags and are usually heavily coated in salt. The simple option is not to snack at all, but to go out for a walk or run instead. If you really do need something to chew on, you should look for something organic and without too much packaging. Read on to find out more.

Lunch

MAKE YOUR OWN LUNCH **By making your own lunch you will save money and have complete control over what you eat. You can save waste by sprucing up the previous night's dinner, if there is any left. You can also make sure all the ingredients in your lunch, or as many as possible, are locally produced and organic.**

AVOID CLING FILM Cling film may be a neat way of wrapping up your sandwiches, but it is also very wasteful. Throwing a thin sheet of plastic in the bin every time you eat your lunch is bad news for the environment. Some types of cling film also contain phthalates, which have been linked to various health problems, including infertility. Instead, put your sandwiches in a reusable box. Amy Bunting from Northampton says she uses old Chinese-takeaway boxes, which is a clever piece of recycling. What could you use?

REUSE ALUMINIUM FOIL If you wrap your sandwiches in foil, fold it up afterwards, take it home and reuse it to wrap the next day's lunch. If it really has run its course, recycle it. Every year 26,000 tonnes of aluminium foil is used in the UK, but just 33% of this is recycled, despite the fact that aluminium is probably the most cost-effective material to recycle. As well as reducing landfill, recycling aluminium requires only 5% of the energy and produces only 5% of the CO_2 emissions compared with its primary production. Aluminium can also be recycled indefinitely, as reprocessing does not damage its structure. You can also close the loop by buying recycled foil from an eco-shop such as **www.naturalcollection.com**.

CUT OUT MEAT Vegetarians and vegans have long campaigned for their cause on the grounds of animal cruelty, but the increased awareness of environmental issues is giving them grounds to change tack. Put simply, eating a vegetarian diet is better for the planet. Meat production requires more resources – land, water, pesticides (to grow feed crops) – to produce the same amount of food as grain or vegetable production.

On top of that, the methane produced by the world's billions of flatulent cows and sheep is one of the primary causes of global warming. Modern farming has also led to diseases being passed from animals to humans through meat consumption, such as BSE and bird flu. A vegetarian diet is also less fattening and potentially healthier. And if you think being a vegetarian is all lettuce leaves and carrot sticks, think again. A quick flick through the pages of the *Leith's Vegetarian Bible*, for example, reveals hundreds of pages of delicious dishes, such as quinoa and apricot salad with toasted pine nuts, and millet pilaff with yellow and orange peppers. The Vegetarian Society (**www.vegsoc.org**) will be more than willing to help you transfer to a meat-free diet, advising on where to find exciting new recipes and answering any health queries you might have.

GET YOUR SANDWICHES DELIVERED BY EMISSIONS-FREE BIKE If your office is out of the way and there is no canteen, consider arranging for a sandwich bike to pass by each morning, before you and your colleagues feel the urge to jump in your cars in search of provisions. If you work in London, try Darwin's Deli (**www.darwinsdeli.co.uk**).

SANDWICH SHOPS If you have to venture out in search of your lunch, try to find somewhere that makes healthy, freshly prepared lunches, rather than buying sandwiches that have been pre-prepared in a factory somewhere. Avoid excess packaging by refusing plastic bags and try to avoid frequenting places that serve everything in separate plastic boxes, with great wads of napkins. Opt for a vegetarian option and if you can find an organic shop, use it.

SIT-DOWN LUNCH We discuss eating out in more detail in chapter 10, but the main principles are to choose an establishment with good eco-credentials, serving organic produce and sustainably caught fish. Ask about the restaurant's recycling policy, and if it doesn't have one make a note not to go back. And if you order a glass of water, make sure it's tap water, not bottled water.

JUICE AND CORDIALS We all know fruit juice is healthy, but the type of fruit juice you buy can make a big difference to the planet. Firstly, many juices are made from exotic fruits, such as pineapple or mango, which have to be transported from the other side of the world. Choose locally produced apple or pear juice, instead. Locally produced cordials include elderflower and blackcurrant. Secondly, if you can, plump for organic juice as it means less pesticides being sprayed over the countryside, contaminating the soil and rivers. Also, fresh juice is healthier than juice 'made from concentrate', although it is also more expensive and needs to be refrigerated. For some tasty organic, UK-produced juices and cordials try Luscombe Organics (**www.luscombe.co.uk**), Belvoir (**www.belvoirfruitfarms.co.uk**), or James White Organics (**www.jameswhite.co.uk/organics.html**).

RECYCLE JUICE CARTONS There is a commonly held belief in the UK that the cartons juice and milk comes in, which are mainly made by Tetra Pak, are not recyclable. However, this is not the case and more and more recycling schemes will now accept them. For a list of areas in the UK where local authorities will recycle cartons, visit **www.tetrapakrecycling. co.uk**. If you are in doubt, contact your local council.

Tea break

GET A BOILING WATER UNIT **If your office goes through a lot of tea and coffee, rather than constantly boiling cold water in a small kettle, suggest installing a wall-mounted boiling water unit. These units can use up to 60% less energy than kettles. As the water is already boiling, it also saves a lot of time, particularly on large tea rounds – which should please your bosses. It is estimated that in an office**

**with 20 staff, two hours a day is spent waiting for the kettle
to boil. Of course, your unit will only be efficient if you turn it
off at night and during the weekend. Take responsibility for
turning it off before you leave each evening.**

BUY FAIRTRADE COFFEE The Fairtrade movement began with
coffee almost 20 years ago. The aim then was the same as it is today, to
give growers a fair price for their coffee beans. It means the end-product
may cost slightly more, but it comes without the aroma of exploitation
or enforced poverty. The Fairtrade label (**www.fairtrade.org.uk**) applies
the same principles to many other products that have traditionally been
produced at the expense of poor workers on farms in the developing
world. These include snack foods such as tea, sugar, nuts and fruit juices.

DON'T SMOKE OK, I know this is easier to say than do, but did you
know that smoking is not only bad for you and others around you, it's also
bad for the planet? For a start, huge amounts of land are cleared to grow
tobacco in parts of the world where food is scarce. The tobacco growers
use huge amounts of pesticides and fertilisers (more than they would
be allowed to use on food crops). These harmful chemicals can get into
drinking water, animals and other crops. Curing tobacco requires it to be
heated, usually by burning wood. Each year, almost 600 million trees are
felled around the world for this purpose. Then there are the vast quantities
of paper required. Each cigarette-manufacturing machine uses four miles
of paper an hour. Is all this really a good use of the world's precious
resources? Then, when it is burned, a cigarette gives off a concoction
of harmful chemicals (cigarette smoke contains over 4,000 chemicals),
including two of the main gases related to the greenhouse effect – carbon
dioxide and methane – as well as over 43 carcinogens. For advice on how
to give up, visit **www.gosmokefree.co.uk** or **www.newash.org.uk**.

UGLY BUTTS A cigarette butt can take up to 12 years to break down,
but many smokers throw them on the floor without a thought. Since the
smoking ban in all work places, if you are a smoker you'll almost certainly
be smoking outside, so rather than use the street, flower beds or lawn as a

bin, carry a 35mm film canister with you to store discarded filters until you can dispose of them properly.

TAKE A FRESH-AIR BREAK Smokers are unfairly permitted a five-minute jaunt outside the building every few hours to satisfy their nicotine craving, while non-smokers are expected to sit and quietly get on with their work. Rebalance this inequality by taking fresh-air breaks. Five minutes away from your desk is good for your eyes, will prevent you from getting repetitive strain injury and will increase your overall productivity. Smokers often claim that their best creative thinking occurs during fag breaks. Well, the same is true of fresh-air breaks.

TOP TIP – LOW IMPACT LIVING INITIATIVE
WORK LESS

You can make possibly the most important difference in your working life by reducing the number of hours you work each week, earning less, spending less and doing something else with your time that is good for the environment, makes you happier and healthier and saves you money (which is handy, because you won't have as much). For example, grow organic vegetables in your garden or allotment; install renewable or energy-saving technology at home; go on a cycling holiday in the UK instead of flying abroad; install a wood stove and split your own logs; keep chickens; do DIY; knit yourself a jumper; go mackerel fishing; collect wild food; brew your own beer; harvest rainwater; start a compost heap; make biodiesel; join a local green group; see your friends more; have a lie-in; climb a tree; make love... you get the picture.

BOYCOTT NESTLÉ Nestlé has been tapping into the tea break market for years. Its Kit Kat chocolate bar has been using the slogan 'Have a break, have a Kit Kat' since 1957. Then there is Nescafé, probably drunk in most offices in the UK. However, despite its ongoing presence at tea breaks everywhere, Nestlé is the most boycotted company in the UK. The ire of campaigners stems from the company's aggressive marketing of baby formula in the developing world. Apart from the many nutritional and emotional benefits of breastfeeding, in parts of the world where the quality of drinking water is poor it can be fatal to switch unnecessarily from breast milk to formula milk. According to UNICEF, a non-breastfed child living in disease-ridden and unhygienic conditions is up to 25 times more likely to die of diarrhoea and four times more likely to die of pneumonia than a breastfed child. It estimates that 1.5 million infants die each year because they are not breastfed. The Boycott Nestlé campaign has been running since 1977 and is still going strong. For details visit **www.babymilkaction.org**. It might make you rethink your choice of coffee and chocolate.

Screen break

BECOME A DESKTOP CAMPAIGNER **If you have to give yourself a quick break from a tedious spreadsheet or database, rather than surfing for the latest gossip on Posh and Becks, become a WWF campaigner. WWF has set up a website to allow you to take direct action on specific issues from the comfort of your desktop. Through the website you can send emails, petitions or faxes to key decision-makers, or edit and print letters to post to targets more responsive to mail. Alternatively, you can send letters of support to campaigners in the field, or sign up to make a personal commitment, such as to buy only FSC-certified wood. According to WWF, online campaigners have already scored a number of successes, including helping ban 'set net' fishing in parts of New Zealand to protect the critically endangered Maui's dolphin, and stopping a plan to hunt and kill all tigers in the northern Malaysian state of Kelantan. To add your voice, visit www.passport.panda.org.**

GIVE YOURSELF A DESK MASSAGE If staring at the screen all day gets you feeling stressed and tight around the shoulders and neck, take two minutes out to give yourself a desk massage. These tips come courtesy of the Stress Management Society (**www.stress.org.uk**):

Sit comfortably with your back supported against the back of the chair, feet firmly on the ground and hands and arms open and relaxed.

1. With a deep breath in, raise the shoulders towards the ears and hold them raised for a few seconds. Then slowly breathe out and drop the shoulders. Repeat several times.

2. Place your left hand on your right shoulder. Squeeze gently and then release. Repeat down the right arm to the elbow. Repeat several times. Place your right hand on your left shoulder and repeat the exercise.

3. Place the fingers of both hands at the base of your skull; apply slow circular pressure down from the base of the skull to the base of the neck.

4. Now close your eyes and relax your face muscles. Be aware of your eye muscles, your jaw and your forehead. Place the fingers of both hands on each of the temples and slowly massage in circular motion. Repeat several times.

5. Finish by cupping your hands over your eyes and holding for several seconds. This helps to release tension and tightness in the face.

CALL IN THE PROFESSIONALS For a more serious de-stressing, tension-relieving massage, call in the experts. There are many companies that will come in to your office and give you a 20-minute massage at your desk. No, you won't have to strip off in front of your colleagues; these massages are fully clothed and without oils, so you can stay sitting in your chair. If you don't want to fork out the money for your own massage, perhaps you can convince your boss of the benefits of a desk massage. These include a less-stressed, and hence healthier, workforce, which leads to higher productivity levels and less time off sick. It can also boost staff morale. For more information, visit **www.stress.org.uk** or **www.aosm.co.uk**.

YOGA Yoga, too, can help stressed office workers relax and feel healthier and happier – bosses take note. Like a massage, yoga can also be done without leaving your desk. Officeyogi (**www.officeyogi.com**) will come to your office and run any of a variety of yoga and meditation classes, including desk yoga and yoga classes designed specifically for men.

GO FOR A WALK If you spend most of your day sitting down, go for a walk at lunchtime. As well as having many health benefits, it will help you get to know your local community a bit better. If while you're out and about you discover that your local area is not very accommodating to walkers, don't give up. The organisation Living Streets (**www.livingstreets. org.uk**) campaigns for better pedestrian access in Britain's towns and cities. Why not lend your support and see if it can help you improve facilities in your local area?

GO FOR A RUN Running is one of the most eco-friendly forms of exercise because it requires no specialist kit apart from a pair of shorts and some trainers. Running is great for losing weight and relieving stress. Try to run in parks or along canals and rivers rather than along main roads to avoid breathing in harmful traffic fumes. If you are really keen, you could even run to and from work, cutting your commuting emissions down to virtually zero.

GET YOURSELF SOME ETHICAL TRAINERS If you are going to take part in some daily exercise, you will probably need to invest in a pair of trainers. The unethical practices of many sports footwear firms have been well documented and, as a result, a number of specialist ethical trainer companies have been started to cater for eco-minded consumers. Ethletic (**www.ethletic.com**) and Worn Again (**www.wornagain.co.uk**) both score highly in *Ethical Consumer* magazine's ethical charts. If you need a specialist running shoe, the most ethical company is New Balance (**www.newbalance.co.uk**), which has a good record on 'pollution and toxics' and makes its trainers in the UK.

SWIMMING Swimming is great exercise, but immersing yourself in a pool full of chemicals has its disadvantages, too. We have all experienced the sore eyes you get after swimming without goggles, but chlorine has also been linked to other ailments, including asthma in children. If you were to buy a bottle of chlorine – if you were lucky enough to have your own pool, for instance – you would notice the long list of warnings on the packaging, including: 'Harmful to aquatic organisms, may cause long-term adverse effects in the aquatic environment'.

Snack time

BUY FAIRTRADE CHOCOLATE In the UK, we just love chocolate and spend almost £4 billion on it each year. However, only a tiny fraction of that spend ends up with

the cocoa farmers who produce it – the average UK family spends more on chocolate in a year than an average cocoa farmer earns in that time. One way to redress this extreme imbalance and to provide growers with a living wage is to buy Fairtrade chocolate. There are many tasty Fairtrade varieties available (such as Divine's dark chocolate bar – divinechocolate.com). For a full list visit www.fairtrade.org.uk.

BEYOND FAIRTRADE Equitrade takes the idea of Fairtrade one step further. While Fairtrade guarantees to pay a fair price to third-world producers of raw materials, such as the farmers who grow cocoa to make chocolate, Equitrade guarantees a fair price for finished products made in developing countries, such as the actual bars of chocolate, or the jars of coffee. In this way, a much higher percentage of the profits stay in the country of origin. One of the leading lights of the Equitrade movement is the Madagascan firm Malagasy (**www.malagasy.co.uk**), which sells chocolate, tea, coffee and spices not only grown in Madagascar, but packaged, designed and produced there, and exported at a fair price. According to Malagasy, for every fairly-traded chocolate bar sold at £1.70 in the UK, the country of origin will see only about 5p. The rest will end up in the pockets of UK companies. For non-Fairtrade chocolates this percentage is even worse, of course. So, to be better than good, look for the Equitrade logo. Visit **www.equitrade.org**.

UNDER THE BANANA SKIN Bananas may seem like a cheap, healthy snack, but that innocent yellow fruit on your desk is the public face of one of the biggest exploitation stories on Earth, and one that is ongoing. The banana industry is dominated by five international companies whose operations are so huge they dwarf the total export revenues of all the main banana-exporting countries combined. Despite being grown halfway across the world, bananas are the most valuable food product for UK supermarkets – only petrol and lottery tickets outsell them. Despite the huge wealth being generated, plantation workers can earn as little as 50p a day in some countries. On top of that, thousands of indigenous people have been driven off their lands to make way for new plantations, while any form of union activity is banned. Worse still, thousands of tonnes of toxic pesticides have been poured on the plantations – often sprayed from aeroplanes overhead, drenching workers still in the fields. Birth defects and serious illness are common among workers as a result. Rather than give up bananas altogether, which are indeed a healthy snack option, make sure you choose Fairtrade or organic bananas. It may cost you a few pence extra, but it will truly make a difference.

WATER COOLERS If you really need your water cooled, rather than drinking it at room temperature, at least turn your water cooler machine off when you leave at night and turn it on when you get in again in the morning – the water won't go off. If you need the water to be cool as soon as you come in, use a timer so that the machine will be switched on an hour before you arrive. Electric device timers can be bought for a few pounds from most electrical-goods shops, such as Maplin (**www.maplin.co.uk**).

VENDING MACHINES A timer device can also be used to reduce the energy used by vending machines. If you need to convince your bosses about the value of turning the office vending machine off at night, tell them that a typical vending machine will use over £400 of electricity each year if left on 24 hours a day – much more than the cost of a timer device. If you switch it off overnight and at weekends you will save around a tonne of CO_2 each a year.

CAKE TIME If someone in the office brings in cake or chocolates for everyone to eat, take responsibility for making sure as much of the packaging gets recycled as possible. If your office has no facilities for recycling cardboard boxes or plastic bags, take them home with you and put them out with your household recycling.

USE REUSABLE PLATES AND CUTLERY Rather than send a whole set of plastic implements to landfill every time someone brings in some birthday cake, kit your office out with a set of real plates and cutlery, which can be used again and again.

USE RECYCLED CUTLERY You may decide it's not worth buying reusable plates and cutlery. After all, you will need to wash them up each time, which can be a hassle and uses hot water and washing-up liquid. Also, they may get broken and thrown out, negating their environmental advantage over disposable plates. If you do plump for disposable implements, however, choose biodegradable plates and cutlery made from potato or cassava starch (**www.vegware.co.uk**) or from sugar cane, reed or corn starch (**www.ecothefriendlyfrog.co.uk**).

SNACKS TO YOUR DOOR If you're not sure where to buy organic and Fairtrade produce for work parties, meetings, or just afternoon snacks, get them delivered. The Organic Delivery Company (**www.organicdelivery.co.uk**) will deliver a range of environmentally friendly selection boxes, from its fruit box to its office party box full of organic beers and wines.

FIND OUT WHAT'S IN YOUR SNACK Many questionable chemicals are regularly added to food products and then simply listed on the ingredients as an E number. If the full story behind each of these numbers was also listed on the packaging, you would probably stop eating many of your favourite convenience foods. The ingredient E102, for example, looks harmless enough. But this is tartrazine, an additive linked to hyperactive behavioural disorder in children, as well as migraines, blurred vision and purple skin patches. Although banned in Norway and Austria, E102 is widely used as a colouring in the UK. To find out the story behind all the other E numbers, visit **www.ukfoodguide.net/enumeric.htm**.

DON'T SNACK Of course, you can save all the potentially harmful consequences of eating a snack by not eating one. This will save production energy, transport emissions and waste, and you may also lose some weight. Going on a diet is hardly the most effective way to save the planet, but it can help. Shedding three and a half stones, for example, will improve the fuel efficiency of your car by 1%, as it will have less weight to carry.

Something for the weekend

Ah, the weekend. Free from the shackles of work, you may not be in the mood to think about putting restrictions on your fun, but, unfortunately, some of our favourite leisure pursuits are contributing to the destruction of the planet. We can't go on ignoring this fact, particularly as it threatens the very existence of some of our favourite activities. European skiing, for example, is threatened by reduced snowfalls, while surfers constantly campaign for cleaner seas. Change should begin with the activities themselves. The surfing industry, for example, has been heavily criticised for using a toxic chemical called toluene diisocyanate to make surfboards. It is now endeavouring to find a suitable eco-friendly alternative. For those with less energetic tendencies, a green weekend needn't mean two days of frugal misery. From turning your garden into a wildlife sanctuary to visiting an organic farm and sampling its produce, there is a long list of leisure pursuits that are fun and help protect the environment.

Go active

GET FIT Being fit and healthy may not benefit the planet directly, but indirectly it can only help. As a nation, our increasingly sedentary and environmentally detrimental habits, such as driving everywhere, watching television and sitting at computers all day, are also linked to the deteriorating state of our health. Between 2003 and 2006, obesity in adults in the UK rose by a staggering 40%. Obesity is responsible for 9,000 premature deaths a year and is a major contributor to heart disease, which is still the leading cause of death in the UK. Exercise can also help alleviate common modern ailments such as stress, backache and sleeplessness. So this weekend, turn off the TV and go and do something less boring and inactive instead.

GREEN SLOPES Ski resorts have a huge incentive to be green as they will almost certainly be among the first victims of global warming. Many ski destinations, particularly lower-altitude resorts, are already struggling to cope with the decreased snowfalls associated with climate change. Unfortunately, most resorts are a long way from being green. In most cases, forests are cut down to make way for pistes. And now, as the snow melts, artificial snow-making machines are being called in more and more to replenish the slopes, burning up vast amounts of energy and draining local water supplies. Then there are the chair-lifts, which also require energy to carry skiers to the tops of the pistes. So what can you do? Well, the best thing would be to not ski at all. If that's too much to bear, try taking one long holiday, rather than lots of weekend trips, to cut down on travel emissions, and if you can, take the train rather than fly – check out **www.eurostar.com/ski** for details. Another thing you can do is choose a resort that is making efforts to be more environmentally friendly. The website **www.saveoursnow.com** rates resorts according to their green credentials, as does **www.skiclub.co.uk/skiclub/resorts/greenresorts**. And if you're feeling fit, consider spending some time cross-country skiing, which doesn't require lifts or large, groomed slopes.

GREEN YOUR GOLF COURSE If you play golf, try to get your local course involved in a wildlife or conservation project. Golf courses can be environmentally damaging, particularly in hot countries such as Spain, where vast amounts of water are required to keep them pristine. However, as large green areas, golf courses can also have a positive impact on nature. Golf courses can be designed and managed so that rather than destroy natural habitats, they become a haven for wildlife. The Sports Turf Research Institute (**www.stri.co.uk**) has an ecology and environmental department dedicated to advising courses on how they can improve their friendliness to wildlife. The R&A, the golf world's rules and development body, provides best practice guidelines for maintaining a sustainable course at **www.bestcourseforgolf.org**.

 CASE STUDY
ED EWING FROM LONDON: FLYING IN ANNECY, NOT TO ANNECY

A paraglider pilot in his spare time, Ed wanted to get away for a few days to test-fly his new glider. He knew that Annecy in France was one of the best places in Europe to fly, but when he looked up flights he found that all the cheap deals were to Geneva, an hour from Annecy. By the time he added up transfer costs and the time getting to and from airports, he realised that the train was the same price, and only an hour's extra journey – eight hours in total. It was a practical decision, but also one coloured by a desire to cut his personal carbon footprint. Yes, we're told that air travel is a small contribution in the grand scheme of things, but actually it is one of the bigger cuts you can make on a personal level. Ed found that the train was easy. He had to take the metro across Paris for two stops – this added an hour to the trip (still eight hours in total). Then a fast TGV all the way to Annecy. Ed left his house at midday on Saturday and by 8.30pm was drinking a whisky in Annecy. Ed discovered that taking the train was a great way to travel. Your holiday starts at the station – you can take your own wine, pack a decent picnic and put your feet up. On a plane it's all hassle, hassle, hassle.

GO SAILING Wind power, that champion of renewable energy, has for centuries been harnessed as a way of transport. And while you may prefer the idea of sailing around in the tropical waters of the Caribbean, you can avoid any carbon-spewing flights by staying in the UK, which offers some of the best sailing in the world. To learn how to sail, contact the UK Sailing Academy (**www.uksa.org**) or the Royal Yachting Association (**www.rya.org.uk**).

JOIN A GREEN GYM Want to get fit without sweating on an electrically powered running machine in front of a giant, energy-consuming TV screen in a brightly lit gym? Green gyms are conservation projects involving regular outdoor work, such as clearing paths and repairing walls and fences. The idea is to help the local environment and to get fit at the same time. For more information and to find your local green gym, visit the British Trust for Conservation Volunteers website at **www.btcv.org/greengym**.

GET AN ALLOTMENT Another way to be green and stay fit is to get an allotment. Not only will you get toned from all that digging, but you'll have fresh, home-grown, organic produce to eat. For help securing your own square of fertile soil visit **www.allotment.org.uk**.

Countryside

EXPLORE THE BRITISH COUNTRYSIDE Cut out the need to fly by taking a weekend break in the UK. From the Scottish Highlands to the smugglers' coves of Cornwall, Britain's countryside is as diverse as it is rich in natural beauty. There are also a growing number of eco-friendly hotels around the country (such as Strattons Hotel in Norfolk, www.strattonshotel.com) and lots of restaurants serving local, seasonal, organic food. For a comprehensive list, try the Soil Association's Organic Directory 2007 (www.soilassociation.org).

GO ORGANIC Discover the benefits of organic food first hand by visiting an organic farm. The Soil Association has created a network of farms open to the public, where you can witness organic farming techniques, taste freshly picked produce in farm cafés or take it home from the farm shop, or just enjoy some fresh country air – free of pesticides, of course. To find an organic farm in your area, visit the Soil Association website (**www.soilassociation.org**) and click on 'Get involved'.

GO FORAGING Don't sit there complaining that organic food is too expensive when it is growing free in woods, hills and hedgerows across the country. From perennial favourites like blackberries and sweet chestnuts, to mushrooms, hazelnuts and sloes, there is a wealth of food out there just waiting to be gathered. Of course, to make sure you don't eat the wrong thing, it helps to know what you're doing. Try going on a short course (see Fergus the Forager at **www.wildmanwildfood.co.uk** or the Wild Food School at **www.countrylovers.co.uk/wfs**), or at the very least reading a book (such as *Food For Free* by Richard Mabey) or magazine (**www.bushcraft-magazine.co.uk**) on the subject.

LEAVE NO TRACE If you go hiking or camping in the wilds, make sure your trip doesn't leave a mark on the environment. Dropping litter doesn't just ruin the beauty of the countryside, it can also be dangerous to wildlife and farm animals and can spread disease. Dropping litter is actually a criminal offence; so take your rubbish home with you. If you are backpacking, plan ahead and bring minimally packaged items to reduce the amount of rubbish you have to carry home with you.

FOLLOW THE COUNTRYSIDE CODE Learn the Countryside Code and stick to it when you venture out and about. The code is split into five key points:

1. Be safe, plan ahead and follow any signs – make sure you have the latest information about where and when you can go and follow any signs and warnings as there may be restricted access, for example, while work is being carried out or during breeding season.

2. Leave gates and property as you find them – don't automatically close every gate, as a farmer may have left it open intentionally.

3. Protect plants and animals and take your litter home – don't remove any rocks or plants as they can provide homes and food for wildlife. Be particularly careful not to drop cigarette butts as they can easily cause devastating fires.

4. Keep dogs under close control – make sure your dog doesn't chase or harm wildlife, farm animals or people. Be warned, farmers are entitled to destroy dogs that injure or even worry their animals. If your dog cannot be trusted, keep it on a lead.

5. Consider other people – drive slowly on country roads, don't block people's drives and keep noise to a minimum.

For more information on the Countryside Code, visit **www.countrysideaccess.gov.uk**.

SPEND YOUR MONEY LOCALLY If you head out on a camping or walking expedition, try to support local communities by buying your supplies in local shops rather than stocking up at a supermarket before you leave. According to the Ramblers' Association (**www.ramblers.org. uk**) spending by walkers in England alone supports up to 231,000 full-time jobs, and no doubt helps many local communities to survive. At the very least, sample the delights of a local pub.

KEEP THE COUNTRYSIDE OPEN When out walking, if you come across a blocked path or other difficulty, such as a broken stile or a path that has been ploughed over, contact your local highway authority (usually the local county council or unitary council), or the Ramblers' Association footpath officer (**www.ramblers.org.uk**) and they will do their best to get the route reopened.

TAKE THE FOOTPATH Statistics from the Audit Commission on England's footpaths show that an average 35% of paths are difficult or impossible to use. If you want to improve the accessibility of England's footpaths, take part in Use Your Footpath Week every June. Visit **www.ramblers.org.uk** for details.

DON'T DRIVE TO WALK Walking is of course a very eco-friendly activity, but if you have to drive to your starting point much of its greenness will be undone. Not being reliant on a car also gives you more flexibility; so you can walk from one place to another, getting a different bus or train there and back, rather than being forced to follow a circular route in order to get back to where you parked your car.

GET GOOD GEAR The world of hiking and camping is full of gadgets and hi-tech clothing and equipment. Try to buy ethically manufactured goods if you can. This is not always easy to do, as a product's ethics are rarely listed on the label. However, *Ethical Consumer* magazine (**www.ethicalconsumer.org**) conducted a survey of the top brands and found that Patagonia (**www.patagonia.com**) came out as the most ethical firm for waterproof jackets and rucksacks, while Ethical Wares (**www.ethicalwares.com**) was the best for hiking boots.

WIND-UP TORCH You've just walked 20 miles in high winds across treacherous mountains, it's getting dark and you need to put your tent up quickly before the rain sets in. You dig around in your rucksack for your torch, pull it out and hey presto, the batteries have run out. Avoid finding out that your only source of light has died just at the precise moment you need it, by getting yourself a wind-up torch. Oh, and by not requiring any batteries it's environmentally friendly, too. Visit **www.winduptorch.co.uk**.

In the garden

GO WILD If you like nothing better than to spend the weekend pottering about in your garden, why not do something to attract some wildlife? Not only are birds, small mammals and insects fascinating

73

to observe, they also rely on gardens to survive. With so much of the country given over to buildings or farmland, gardens provide refuge for much of Britain's wildlife. So, avoid pesticides, slug pellets and other poisonous substances and instead let your garden run a little wild, at least in one corner. Then sit back and watch as nature embraces it.

CHECK BEFORE YOU MOW Every day hedgehogs are killed by people mowing their lawns. Other small animals, such as frogs, also regularly suffer the same terrible fate. Before starting up your mower or strimmer, check the long grass and undergrowth with your hand or foot to make sure nothing is curled up there. Hedgehogs don't run away when they hear the noise, but curl up tightly, which is, unfortunately, no protection against fast-rotating blades. For more information visit **www.thehedgehog.co.uk/strimmers.htm**.

FEED THE BIRDS Putting out some breadcrumbs will attract birds, but for a more permanent attraction, put up a bird feeder or plant some bird-friendly bushes. Bird feeders come in all shapes and sizes depending on which birds you want to attract and whether you need to keep food out of the way of squirrels, who can scare the birds away and eat all the food. Alternatively, planting bushes with berries that birds enjoy, such as ivy or Pyracantha, gives you a natural bird feeder that regularly tops itself up. The Royal Society for the Protection of Birds (RSPB) provides an invaluable source of information on feeding birds. Visit **www.rspb.org.uk/feedthebirds**.

GIVE THEM SHELTER Attract wildlife into your garden by giving it a place to stay. You can buy all sorts of bird boxes, hedgehog houses, ladybird boxes, bee nest boxes, butterfly boxes, bat boxes and even frog and toad houses.

Most of these can be bought from the RSPB, whose shop branches out into the world beyond birds (**www.rspbshop.co.uk**). Or for even greater satisfaction, you could make your own. Instructions on how to build houses for birds and other animals can be found in many books in your local library or bookshop, or on many sites online. A good place to start is your local Wildlife Trust – visit **www.wildlifetrusts.org**.

SET UP A BIRD BATH Birds need water to bathe in, especially over the winter. They use the water for preening, which helps to oil their feathers and so provide waterproofing and insulation against the winter cold. If you don't fancy a Sunday afternoon trip to your local garden centre to buy a nice custom-made bird bath, you can always improvise by simply using a wide, shallow bowl. Then, find a nice clean window and watch the fun take place.

GET A CAT DETERRENT To prevent birds and small mammals being killed or attacked while playing in your garden, you can install an electric cat deterrent device. A survey by the Mammal Society found that cats kill at least 250 million creatures in Britain every year. The RSPB recommends getting the Catwatch deterrent (**www.rspbshop.co.uk**), which has a sensor that detects movement up to 12 metres away and then emits a sound (silent to humans) pitched specifically at a cat's hearing frequency, which will deter the cat without harming it.

MAKE A WOOD PILE You can attract a whole host of creatures into your garden by leaving a pile of logs in a damp, shady corner of your garden. Hedgehogs, frogs, toads or newts may spend the winter there, while centipedes and ground and rove beetles, which eat slugs, may also be attracted to it. Another visitor may be the stag beetle, a globally threatened species that likes to lay its eggs near dead wood or logs. The larvae live in the wood for several years until they reach maturity, so leaving the pile undisturbed is vital.

BUILD A POND A pond is possibly the most vital part of any wildlife garden. A pond may attract frogs, toads, newts, dragonflies and even snakes. You can make your own or buy prefabricated ones from your local garden centre. Put your pond somewhere sunny to attract the greatest variety of wildlife, and avoid positioning it near a tree so you don't have to spend the entire autumn clearing out fallen leaves. Make sure your pond has a least one gently sloping side so that amphibians and mammals can get out easily. A variety of depths will provide the greatest number of habitats, and ideally one section of the pond should be at least 60cm deep to provide a refuge for pond creatures if the water freezes over.

MAKE A COMPOST HEAP Make use of your kitchen scraps and your garden waste by turning them into compost that will one day feed and mulch your soil. Not only is this a more sustainable way to deal with some of the waste we generate, it also provides a warm and sheltered environment for many mini-beasts and for their predators, such as frogs and hedgehogs. A heap rather than a bin will also allow birds to feed off any suitable invertebrates. The basic principle of making a compost heap is to mix 'greens' (grass clippings, kitchen waste, soft prunings) with 'browns' (cardboard, dry leaves, woody prunings) to ensure a good balance of materials rich in nitrogen and carbon.

Time out

ORDER YOUR DRINKS IN A GLASS Environmental concerns may not be at the forefront of your thoughts as you let your hair down on a Friday or Saturday night, but even here, little things can make a difference. For example, if you drink beer, order something on tap rather than asking for a bottle. Although some pubs will recycle used bottles, many don't. And even if they do, it is more eco-friendly to reuse a glass than to recycle a glass bottle.

CASE STUDY
ENVIRO: ELECTRIC MOVES

Rotterdam think-tank Enviro did some research and calculated that an average-sized club consumes 150 times more energy than a family of four each year. It then set about transforming the Rotterdam clubbing scene. Among its ideas were recycling car seats by using them in a cinema, using recycled bicycle handles as door handles and using the sweat from dancers to flush the lavatories. But its pièce de résistance is an electricity-generating dancefloor, which uses the kinetic energy of the dancers on the floor to generate power. Although you are unlikely to find any of these ideas springing up in UK clubs any time soon, if you fancy a cutting-edge, eco-friendly night out in Rotterdam, check out the Sustainable Dance Club (**www.sustainabledanceclub.com**).

GO ON A GREEN DATE If you shudder at the thought of going out with a partner who leaves all the lights on, sprays air freshener everywhere and looks puzzled at the mention of climate change, find your green-minded soul mate by signing up to a green dating agency, such as Natural Friends (**www.natural-friends.com**).

CONDOM ETIQUETTE If you find a partner, don't suddenly forget your green principles in all the excitement. Around 150 million condoms are flushed down UK toilets each year, clogging water treatment filters and causing sewage overflows in rivers and on beaches, so make sure you put them in the bin. For more information, visit **www.bagandbin.org**.

COOK SOME FOOD SLOWLY The slow food movement was started as an antidote to the seemingly unstoppable advance of the fast food industry. The core message of the slow food movement is that time should be taken in the growing and preparing of food, that food should be grown and prepared locally, and that food and the environment are inseparable. If this sounds good to you, why not become a member and join in the many events and eating sessions organised by the movement? To find your local group, visit **www.slowfood.org.uk**.

TURN THE LIGHTS OUT Have an electricity-free weekend. This is best done in the summer when you don't need to go so long without lights. It is a fun thing to do and will help you realise the amount of electricity you use on a daily basis. So, turn everything off. The TV, the radio (unless it's a wind-up one), the lights, the PlayStation – you may want to make an exception with the fridge, unless you have planned ahead and bought food that can survive in a cool corner or bucket of cold water for a few days. Instead, light some candles, eat raw food, read, learn to knit, talk to your family, play an instrument – can you think of anything else?

WATCH *AN INCONVENIENT TRUTH* If you are still wondering what all the fuss is about global warming, watch Al Gore's Oscar-winning documentary *An Inconvenient Truth*. The film led to Al Gore winning the Nobel Peace Prize, and environmental groups have been quick to praise its inspiring nature – Friends of the Earth set up a series of special screenings across the UK. The government, too, has used the film to inform people of the perils of climate change and galvanise them into action. In 2007, the education secretary announced that a copy of the film would be sent to every secondary school. One US blogger is so keen for people to see Gore's film that he has set up a special promotional website (**www.**

sharethetruth.us). If you contact him he will send a free copy to your local library so you can borrow it and watch it for free. He says that apart from, perhaps, saving yourself from a fire there is nothing more urgent you can do in your life than watch this film.

Time off

THINK BEFORE YOU BOOK **Done wrong, your annual holiday could be the most environmentally damaging and unethical thing you do all year. And because it's all dressed up as fun, you may not even realise it. From carbon-spewing flights, to resorts that sap the energy, money and life out of local areas, an irresponsible holiday can undo all the green efforts you make at home in one fell swoop.**

TRAVEL BY LAND OR SEA We don't always have the time to travel by land, particularly to long-haul destinations, but do it where you can. The Oz Bus (**www.oz-bus.com**) from London to Sydney may not be everyone's idea of fun, but for travel to Europe, trains, ferries and buses are often a viable and enjoyable alternative. For timetables, prices and advice on travelling to Europe this way, pay a visit to The Man in Seat 61 (**www.seat61.com**).

NOT EVERYTHING 'ECO' IS ECO 'Eco' is the current buzzword in the travel industry and it is applied liberally with virtually no official restrictions. Many hotels and resorts will claim to be 'eco-hotels' simply because they use some local food in the restaurant or have lights that turn off automatically when you leave the room. While these things are commendable, they are not much use if the same hotel is redirecting the local town's entire water supply to maintain its golf course. So, make sure you look at the details behind any green claims. Ask your tour operator if the resort or hotel you're planning to visit has a written or online environmental policy. Ask what percentage of its employees are local people and whether any of them hold management positions. Does it support any projects that benefit the local environment or community? Has it got an official eco-label or certificate? (These are described in more detail in chapter 9.) Has it won any eco-awards?

USE ECO-FRIENDLY TRAVEL AGENTS You can make sure your holiday is environmentally and culturally sensitive by booking it through a tour operator or website specialising in ethical travel, such as **www.responsibletravel.com**.

BOYCOTT BURMA It may be a beautiful place with luxury hotels, but Burma is also a country run by one of the world's most oppressive military dictatorships. The military junta in control of the country promotes tourism in the hope of garnering international credibility and making money. However, most of Burma's resorts were built with forced labour, and the imprisoned leader of the pro-democracy opposition in Burma, Aung San Suu Kyi, is just one of many voices calling for tourists to boycott the country. She says: 'Burma will be here for many years, so tell your friends to visit us later. Visiting now is tantamount to condoning the regime.' For more information, visit **www.burmacampaign.org.uk/tourism.php**.

USE NATURAL INSECT REPELLENT Getting bitten by insects abroad is not only extremely annoying and often painful, but it can cause serious illness, too. So most of us, not willing to take any chances, head straight to the chemist and ask for the strongest thing they've got. Many of these products, however, are full of highly toxic chemicals. The most common of these is DEET, which is a recognised pesticide and has been linked to health problems in humans, and fish if it gets into rivers. It's not really the kind of thing you want to be rubbing into your skin. Instead, plump for a natural repellent made from essential oils, many of which are just as effective. In addition, wear long-sleeved tops and keep covered, particularly at times when the mosquitoes are busiest, such as during rainy seasons. And at night, sleep under a mosquito net.

CONSERVE AT HOME Possibly the greenest holiday you can take is to join a UK-based conservation project. This doesn't have to mean picking litter by the side of a motorway. The Wildlife Trusts (**www.wildlifetrusts.org**) run basking shark holidays, for example, where you spend five days at sea working alongside scientists gathering information to help protect the sharks. Or you could try learning the art of dry stone walling on a National Trust holiday (**www.nationaltrust.org.uk**).

Moving on up

Reduce the environmental impact of your daily working life in one big swoop by changing jobs. You may be green at home, recycling everything down to your old toothbrushes, but it will all be slightly undermined if you work for a company drilling for oil in the Alaskan wilderness. While applying for a position in the growing environmental sector, such as in renewable energy or recycling, is the most obvious way to green your job, environmental concerns cross over all industries and sectors. Every department can do its bit to be green, from the cleaners to the managing directors. And it doesn't necessarily mean donning your wellies and heading outside either. Most environmental jobs are office based, from setting up energy-saving schemes to vetting planning regulations. And as it is unlikely that the world's environmental problems are going to disappear overnight, it is a sector that does, unfortunately, offer long-term prospects.

Career change

FIRST, BE SURE **Changing your career is a big step and you should be sure it is what you want to do, as it will require effort and sacrifice. Make sure it really is your career, and not just your job, or your hours, or your boss, that you want to change. And make sure it isn't the case of just a bad day in the office. Have you been feeling like this for a while? Can you talk to your line manager or HR department about flexible hours, or an increase in your responsibilities? If it really is the need to be greener that is driving your decision, have you tried implementing environmental schemes in your current workplace, such as putting out recycling boxes? Your colleagues may be more receptive than you think.**

SHORT COURSE Once you have made the decision to change your career for something greener, the best approach is often to start with small steps rather than just quitting your job and then wondering what to do next. Depending in which area you want to work, it may be useful to do an evening or weekend course. Try contacting your local university or college of higher education and asking to see a list of part-time courses they offer. The Open University (**www.open.ac.uk**), too, offers a way of studying while you work. For a more hands-on course, such as alternative building methods or how to convert your engine to run on vegetable oil, try the Centre for Alternative Technology (**www.cat.org.uk**) in Wales, or the Low Impact Living Initiative (**www.lowimpact.org**), which runs short courses on things like self-building a solar hot water system and preserving food.

WELL MANAGED The Institute of Environmental Management and Assessment runs training courses for those managing, implementing and assessing a company's environmental policy. As we mention repeatedly throughout this book, the better you do this, the better for you (in terms of improving your skills, performance and job satisfaction), the better for your company (bigger savings, better PR and staff morale), and, of course, the better for the planet. So, to put your name down for some professional training visit **www.iema.net/training**.

VOLUNTEER Many vacancies in the environmental sector attract fierce competition, so you need to do everything in your power to improve your chances of securing a coveted position. One of the best ways to do this is to volunteer. Doing this demonstrates to potential employers that you are committed to the sector. It will also give you valuable experience in your chosen field. It will also give you a foot in the door – you are likely to be the first to hear of any potential vacancies, as you will already be working there, and, if you make a good impression, you will be at the top of the list of potential candidates. And, finally, volunteering will help you decide if this really is the career for you, as you will get to see it at first hand. To find out about volunteering opportunities, visit Community Service Volunteers (**www.csv.org.uk**), do-it (**www.do-it.org.uk**) or Volunteering England (**www.volunteering.org.uk**).

FLEXIBLE ARRANGEMENTS You may feel that volunteering is a good idea, but that you cannot afford to give up work to do it. However, it doesn't have to be something you do full time. If you can arrange with your boss to work flexible hours, you may be able to start and finish work earlier, for example, and volunteer after work. Or you may be able to cut your hours down slightly, to say four days a week, and then volunteer on the other day.

DO AN INTERNSHIP An internship is a bit like volunteering, although it is usually full time and you usually spend time learning about an organisation's various roles – whereas in volunteering you are usually given a specific job to actually do. Internships can be hard to find, and even harder to secure, but they do exist, so contact favoured organisations and ask them if they run an intern scheme. One that does, for example, is the International Fund for Animal Welfare (**www.ifaw.org**). Interns on its Song of the Whale programme spend three weeks at sea researching whales with a team of scientists.

LONG COURSE If you have the means and the inclination to retrain, you may find a full-time course is the best way forward. The Graduate School of the Environment, part of the Centre for Alternative Technology, runs two post-graduate Msc courses and a professional diploma in architecture. Visit **gradschool.cat.org.uk/graduateschool**. Alternatively, look up the courses available at your local higher or further education establishment.

LOOK AT JOB ADS A good way to find out what skills or qualifications you should be looking to obtain is to read interesting job ads to see what potential employers are looking for in candidates. This will give you a better idea of which courses or volunteering positions you should apply for.

TIGHTEN YOUR BELT If you are going to cut down your hours to do some shadow work, volunteering or a short course, you will need to consider the financial implications of a reduced salary. You may have to budget for a while, move back in with your parents or rely on your partner for support as most of the government's financial support for retraining is focused on unemployed workers rather than those wishing to change career. If you are changing career for the benefit of the planet and for your own personal fulfilment, a drop in earnings may be something you have already accepted as a price worth paying.

ACQUIRE ADDITIONAL SKILLS Don't write off the value of unconnected skills. You are unlikely to be the only applicant with the right qualifications and experience for a particular job, so other skills may give you an advantage. Things like computer or language skills, for example, may prove beneficial, depending on the vacancy.

NETWORK A surprising number of paid jobs in the environmental sector are never advertised. Some evolve through volunteer posts, while many others are filled by personal contact or word of mouth. And to be the person they contact requires networking. Join the association or society representing your chosen area and attend any networking events or conferences they host. Talk to people already working in the field and see if you can arrange to shadow them for a day.

WHERE DO YOU FIT IN? There are five main areas of work for environmental professionals, each with its different pros and cons, working cultures and rewards. The five areas are:

1. Consultancies – this is a growth area with lots of opportunities for those with experience, advising companies on how to be green. There are also opportunities to branch out on your own.

2. Industry – the type and level of environmental work in the private sector is hugely varied depending on the industry and the company. Many firms will employ somebody junior for the task of implementing environmental policies, or give the responsibility to a current employee to do alongside another job. Other firms will recognise the benefits of employing a separate environmental manager or legal expert.

3. Public sector – these are the regulators and policy-makers. There is good job security and as the government takes its role on protecting the environment ever more seriously, the opportunities in this area will grow.

4. Voluntary sector – in many ways this is the glamourous end of environmental work. These are the organisations pushing the agenda, urging companies and the government to be green, and working at the front line of environmental work. The downside is that wages are generally lower in this sector.

5. Education – as well as teaching future generations about protecting the environment, the education sector, through universities, is responsible for much of the research into the state of the environment that has led us to the point where we even realise we are damaging it.

Gis a job

BE PROACTIVE Many green industries, such as renewable energy, are relatively new and exciting and so vacancies are usually filled quickly and easily, often without the need for firms to advertise them. **To give yourself a chance of finding a position, take a proactive approach by researching the market and approaching relevant companies directly. Send in your CV and follow up with a phone call – and be prepared for that to turn into an interview.**

USE A SPECIALIST RECRUITMENT AGENCY Talk to a specialist recruitment agency dealing with the environmental sector about your prospects and aspirations. As well has having lists of vacancies, agencies will be able to look at your CV and give you advice as to which areas you may be able to find work, and how to go about it. There are lots of agencies out there, such as Evergreen Resources (**www.evergreen. org.uk**) and Hunt Blue (**www.huntblue.com**).

LOOK ONLINE Many environmental vacancies are advertised with specialist online job searches such as **www.endsjobsearch.co.uk**, **www. acre-resources.co.uk**, **www.ecojobs.com** or **www.greenjobsonline. co.uk**. You will also find job adverts in the relevant sections of *The Guardian* and *The Independent* newspapers, as well as in specialist magazines.

CHOOSE YOUR EMPLOYER CAREFULLY 'Where do you work? What? Sorry, I didn't catch that. Hey, come back.' Avoid getting embarrassed when someone asks you where you work by not working for a company with a bad ethical reputation. To find out about the environmental record of prospective employers, check out their websites to see if they have an ethical or environmental policy. Another technique is to 'Google' them to see what comes up. To do this, simply type the company's name into the search engine **www.google.com** – although don't believe everything you read about them, not everything on the internet is true, particularly on personal websites or blogs. The website Corp Watch (**www.corpwatch.org**) reports on companies with poor environmental or ethical records, so check to see if your employer is listed. If you have any doubts about companies, ring them up to ask about them, as they may be making efforts to improve.

MAKE A POSITIVE CHOICE If you are concerned about the plight of the planet, you will feel happier working at a company that has facilities for you to cycle to work, provides organic food in its canteen and recycles everything. Factor in a company's environmental policies along with the salary, the hours and the location of the office when deciding where to work.

ASK ABOUT GREEN POLICY IN INTERVIEWS For many companies, improving their eco-practices are as much about attracting high-quality staff as improving public relations, so if you are applying for a job with a company with a low public profile, and you are unsure of its environmental policy, ask about it in your interview. If it takes the environment seriously, your interviewers will be impressed with your questioning. If not, you may not want to work for them anyway.

ASK ABOUT GREEN OPPORTUNITIES IN INTERVIEWS If you are the type of person who likes to get involved in environmental activities, ask what opportunities will be available to you when you join a firm. Again, if they try to brush you off, this may not be the firm for you. On the other hand, if you keep your questioning positive, such as asking if you would be authorised to implement cost-saving energy-efficiency measures, you may find them jumping to offer you the position.

START YOUR OWN ECO-BUSINESS

With the green industry still relatively young, there are still lots of gaps in the market to be plugged. Being green is also particularly compatible with small-scale businesses – which can more easily control their environmental impact – and so it is an area ripe for new ventures. Just a quick look at any eco-list will reveal very few major brands or labels – although they are trying to muscle in slowly. If you are thinking of starting your own

eco-business, get some advice on how to go about it from organisations such as Striding Out (**www.stridingout.co.uk**) or Start Business (**www.startbusiness.co.uk**).

GET SOME HELP The more ethical your business, the more likely it is that you may be able to get some funding to help get started. The Esmee Fairbairn Foundation (**www.esmeefairbairn.org.uk**), for example, offers grants to organisations taking an entrepreneurial approach to tackling social needs. Other organisations providing funding to social enterprises are the Big Issue Invest (**www.biginvest.co.uk**), the government-financed organisation Tackling Social Exclusion in Rural England (**www.enterprise4inclusion.org.uk**) and UnLtd (**www.unltd.org.uk).**

STAY WHERE YOU ARE If being green is important to you, you don't necessarily have to switch to an environmental organisation. Take this book and use the advice in it to turn the company you work at green. It doesn't matter if you are an architect, a doctor or a worker in a fast-food restaurant, every company can do something to be greener – in fact, the less ethical and environmentally conscious your company, the more room for improvement, and any changes you do manage to influence will be all the more important and valuable.

Help your career

SAVE YOUR COMPANY MONEY Virtually every business has the same primary aim, to make money. So how can your employer fail to be impressed if you manage to save the company money through suggesting changes to its environmental practices, such as becoming more energy efficient, or improving the company's public image?

CALLING ALL PAS Some jobs are more suited to taking on additional, company-wide responsibilities than others. PAs, for example, often have some spare time, are good at diplomacy – often needed when asking employees to make green changes – and usually have the ear of someone senior within the company. By taking on the responsibility to encourage environmental change within the company, PAs can gain valuable project management and management reporting skills, and show their initiative – attributes that will come in handy when applying for more responsibility or a job promotion. Recognising the mutual benefits of PAs taking responsibility for green developments, employment agency Reed runs a two-day course called The Green PA and Office Manager. Visit **www.reedlearning.co.uk/green**.

TAKE A GREEN SABBATICAL If your company offers you a sabbatical, use it to make a difference. Volunteer on a social or environmental project, such as the marine conservation and wildlife research expeditions in Africa and Latin America organised by Global Vision International (**www.gvi.co.uk**). Not only can these projects be wildly exciting, but they can be vital for sustainable development in some of the poorest parts of the world.

TOP TIP – TIMEBANK
GIVE TIME TO GO GREEN

Your time is precious. We know it's a lot to ask you to spend it volunteering, but you don't have to give up your free time. You can ask your boss to set up an employee volunteering scheme and do it on their time instead. From walking an elderly person's dog to mentoring a young person in care, coaching a sports team, conducting tours of a stately home or undertaking beach surveys of coastal flora and fauna, there's bound to be something to interest you. For more information about volunteering visit **www.timebank.org.uk** or call 0845 601 4008.

A WORD OF CAUTION Before jetting off on some adventure with the intention of helping those less well off in some far flung corner of the globe, make sure you vet the scheme you are joining. Voluntary Services Overseas recently criticised the growth of what it called 'charity tourism' – profit-making companies sending people on volunteering projects that end up doing more harm than good, particularly when you factor in the CO_2 produced from the flight there. Websites such as **www.ethicalvolunteering.org** can help you critically examine any volunteering schemes you may be considering. Check what training you will receive, whether local people will be involved in running the project, what proportion of the money you pay goes to the communities you are helping and whether the project delivers lasting and sustainable benefits.

TOP TIP – BTCV
INSPIRE YOUR TEAM THE GREEN WAY

Take part in an Employee Action Day with BTCV and leave a lasting legacy for your local area. Employee volunteering helps improve the natural landscape and provides participants with active, outdoor experiences as they work together in ways they haven't before. Tasks range from dry stone walling in beautiful countryside, creating a nature area in school grounds and regeneration of an area of urban wasteland to planting trees in local woodland. Visit **www.btcv.org** or contact customer services on 01302 388883 for further details.

The Workplace

Office politics

Most offices constantly whirr and hum with the sound of inefficient machinery. Running archaic systems set up in the days before you became concerned with saving energy, these computers, printers, fax machines – even fridges and water coolers – waste company money and damage the environment. Your more conscientious colleagues may turn their computers off at night, but to achieve real change you need to look at the systems and processes on which your workplace is built, the attitude towards saving energy and the entire office environment. It is actually, in most cases, quite easy and mutually beneficial. It is what environmentalists call the 'low-hanging fruit', the stuff that is easy to change and will save you money.

Saving energy

GET OUT THE MEASURING STICK We've been told many times that saving energy will also save us money, but it often seems hard to quantify. Will turning off lights and computers really save anything more than a few pennies? Well, why not find out? Rather than rely on general statistics, calculate how much energy your company uses and how much it costs before implementing any energy-saving measures. Then, afterwards, look at the difference. Even easier is to install a monitoring device, such as the Owl (www.theowl.com). This measures the amount of electricity in use at any one moment and shows you the cost saving and reduction in CO_2 emissions every time you turn something off.

GET OUT THE TRACKER For a more detailed breakdown of your energy use, Doctor Energy (**www.doctorenergy.co.uk**) produces a range of Energy Tracker devices to monitor electricity usage, humidity and temperature throughout the workplace – the devices will even sound an alarm if your set thresholds are exceeded. Doctor Energy can also provide

an even more detailed infrared thermography survey, which produces a visual infrared scan of your workplace and highlights exactly where heat, and hence energy, is being produced and where it is being lost.

GET A CARBON TRUST SURVEY Environmental charity the Carbon Trust will come into your office or place of work and review your energy use. The chances are it will save you money and reduce your carbon emissions. After a visit from the Carbon Trust, Westbury Dairies, which had an annual energy bill of £2 million, was told it could save £400,000 a year and reduce its emissions by a sixth. For companies with an annual energy bill of over £50,000, the Carbon Trust will conduct its survey for free. To apply, call 0800 085 2005 or visit **www.carbontrust.co.uk**.

SMALL DETAILS If you don't have time for a full audit of your energy usage, at the very least get a detailed electricity bill from your supplier. This is a breakdown of how much electricity you use and when, and may help you spot times of unnecessary usage, such as in the middle of the night.

KIT YOUR OFFICE OUT WITH INTELLIPANELS Intellipanels are energy-saving multi-plugs. They automatically register when a PC is on and allow power to peripherals such as printers and scanners. If the PC shuts down, they automatically shut down the peripherals, too, which often get left on even though they can't be used independently. This takes the burden of saving energy off the shoulders of those forgetful colleagues who, no matter how many notices you post on the intranet, still leave their printers on overnight. Intellipanels are available from One Click (**www.oneclickpower.co.uk**).

TURN THE HEATING DOWN Workers will complain if it's too cold, but they won't feel comfortable if it's too hot either. In many businesses heating can account for around 60% of total energy bills. We've all been told the blindingly obvious fact that turning the thermostat down 1˚C will reduce energy, but what is the best temperature to work at? This will depend on personal preferences, but generally in offices you shouldn't need to set it any higher than 20˚C. In workshops and storerooms where physical work takes place this can be a lot lower, around 12°C. If you find your workers opening windows because they're too hot, turn the heating down.

HEAT REFLECTOR Up to 70% of the heat from the back of a radiator is used to heat the wall behind it. Get this wasted heat back by sticking a reflective radiator panel down there, which will bounce the heat back into the room, or at least back into the radiator. Obviously, this will mean that your heating system won't have to work so hard to keep your building warm, saving energy and reducing your heating bill. Heatkeeper radiator panels are available in packs of 20 from Green & Easy (**www.greenandeasy.co.uk**).

CASE STUDY
ENI

Staff at Italian energy giant, Eni, were told to leave their ties and suits at home during the summer and to wear something more comfortable instead. Repeating an initiative set up by the Japanese government in 2005, the company asked staff if they would be willing to relinquish their standard office attire so that it could turn down the air conditioning, saving money and reducing carbon emissions. Ninety per cent said yes. And these were sharp-dressing Italians. By allowing the building temperature to edge up just 1°C, Eni estimates it will save 217,000 kilowatts per hour, a reduction of 114 tonnes of carbon dioxide released into the atmosphere over the summer, or the amount of carbon emissions that would be saved if 140 employees came to work by public transport rather than private car for a whole year. The nationwide Japanese initiative, by the way, now in its third year, saves an estimated 417,000 tonnes of carbon emissions each summer, according to the country's environment ministry.

HOT AND COLD It may sound obvious, but check your air conditioning thermostats are set higher than your heating so you don't have the wasteful situation where both are running simultaneously in a battle to counteract each other.

OPTIMISE YOUR VOLTAGE Lower the voltage level in your office by installing a voltage power optimiser. This can reduce the voltage of a whole site, reducing energy bills by up to 20% and increasing the efficiency of electrical equipment. Visit **www.powerperfector.com**.

USE ENERGY-SAVING LIGHT BULBS Of all the things you can do to be green, this has probably been the most trumpeted. And with good reason. Ninety per cent of the energy in a standard light bulb is used to create heat, rather than light. All of this wasted energy can be saved by replacing old bulbs with energy-saving varieties. Just changing one light bulb can reduce your energy bill by £60 over the life of the bulb. Imagine how much you could save in an entire office.

INSULATE PIPES We talk about insulation in more depth in Chapter 14, but one thing you can do quickly and easily without calling in the builders is insulate any bare hot water pipes. If you have ever touched one, you'll know how hot they can get, but most of that heat is being lost. Instead, buy some pipe insulation foam strips and put them on wherever you can – the strips are usually split along one side, making them easy to clip on. If they're not the right length, they're easy to cut.

Computers and stuff

GREEN MACHINES **The global IT industry accounts for roughly 2% of global carbon emissions – that's about the same amount as the much-vilified aviation industry. So the type of computer hardware your company purchases will have a significant and lasting environmental impact. Begin by researching the ethical and environmental record of various manufacturers. A good place to do this is on the website** www.gooshing.co.uk**, which is a venture run by the Ethical Company Organisation. It rates and compares computer hardware according to both the price and the company's ethical record.**

AVOID TOXIC COMPUTERS Choose computer hardware that uses fewer toxic chemicals in the manufacturing process. This is not something you can usually do just by looking at the label, however. Helpfully, Greenpeace (**www.greenpeace.org/electronics**) has drawn up a guide ranking manufacturers and listing the worst offenders.

LOOK FOR AN ENERGY STAR Choosing energy-efficient computer hardware is not for the technologically faint-hearted. All those megabytes and gigawatts can make your head spin. Although not yet universal, the Energy Star label (**www.eu-energystar.org**) is increasingly the sign to look for when attempting to purchase efficient electronic equipment. Anything that has earned the Energy Star uses less energy and automatically enters a low-power mode when not in use.

ANOTHER ECO-LABEL TO LOOK FOR The TCO label (**www.tcodevelopment.com**) is a little more complex than Energy Star, but it still works as a guarantee of energy efficiency. It was set up by the Swedish Confederation for Professional Employees and provides labelling standards for a range of office products, from furniture coverings and mobile phones to computer equipment. As well as having fixed criteria for a product's environmental impact, covering power consumption, energy saving, recyclability and the use of hazardous substances during manufacture, the label also takes into account ergonomics and electromagnetic emissions; the intention of the scheme being to provide an all-round symbol of quality.

GET IT SUSSED Before you buy any new computers, laptops, monitors, printers or photocopiers, check out their energy efficiency using the website **www.sust-it.net**. This site rates popular devices according to the amount of energy they use and works out how much each device is likely to cost you to run over the course of a year.

USE A TERMINAL SERVER AND WORKSTATIONS Rather than providing a powerful computer for each person in the office, buy a terminal server and then give each person either an old computer or, even better, a 'thin client' device, both of which use less power. This will save you vast amounts of energy, with substantial cost savings, while users will have access to virtually all the same functionality as before. You may even find that it is faster than the old system. Setting up a terminal server requires a fairly high degree of technical know-how, so ask your IT people about it.

GO FOR A FLAT SCREEN One of the simplest decisions you can make to save energy is to choose a TFT LCD flat-panel model over an older analogue CRT monitor, which requires up to 50% more electricity to run. In fact, older monitors can be consuming almost as much power as the computers they're connected to. CRT models are now almost obsolete if you're buying new, but if you still have them in your office you should consider upgrading. If you do, don't forget to recycle your old monitor (see chapter 8).

BAMBOO MONITORS If you want to show off your eco-credentials with something out of the ordinary, go for a bamboo monitor, mouse and keyboard. Bamboo is a grass and grows quickly, so is an easily renewable raw material that biodegrades much more easily than plastic. However, the steep price means you'll be paying for your eco-statement. Bamboo monitors, keyboards and mice are available from Nigel's Eco Store (**www.nigelsecostore.com**).

CLEAN OUT THE ENGINE ROOM Data centres, the places where larger companies keep their most powerful computer servers, are incredibly wasteful in terms of both energy and money. Filled with vast racks of machines that need to be constantly powered and cooled, the average British data centre uses more energy in a year than the entire city of Leicester. So, what's in yours? Do you even know? Ask tough questions of your data centre manager, such as whether the centre uses the most energy-efficient hardware or has an eco-cooling system of some sort. If it doesn't, find one that does. The Smartbunker data centre, for example, is 100% powered by renewable wind energy and claims its managed servers use 60% less energy than conventional ones (**www.smartbunker.com**).

GO PAPERLESS Despite years of talking about the paperless offices of the future, most companies still unnecessarily print out documents such as invoices and purchase orders to put in the post or to archive in big rooms full of filing cabinets. This is 2008, not 1968. Computer systems can now efficiently archive documents and send invoices by email. Not only does this save on paper and ink, but also the emissions caused by transporting documents and the energy used to keep archive rooms warm and lit.

THE SOFTWARE APPROACH If your IT system is too disorganised to be reliable for archiving, invoicing and all those other processes that usually involve printing things out, you could use a specialised software package to sort it out for you, such as Version One's document management and imaging software (**www.versionone.co.uk**). This will easily scan and safely organise all your documents, and also send out documents electronically. The soft drinks firm Nichols plc, the maker of Vimto, implemented the Version One software in 2003 and says it is now saving £100,000 a year – and no doubt lots of trees and CO_2 emissions.

The work space

HOW CLEAN IS YOUR OFFICE? **When you go home at night, does a team of low-paid cleaners arrive to spray toxic and environmentally damaging chemicals all over your office? The answer is probably yes. But just because you're not there, it doesn't mean you can't do anything about it. Get your cleaners to clean up their act by using eco-products such as those in the Ecover range (www.ecover.com). And if they won't, switch to an eco-cleaning service that does, such as Green Your Office (www.greenyouroffice.co.uk). Green Your Office also has an ethical employment policy to ensure that its cleaning staff are not exploited.**

PENS AND PAPER The average office is strewn with bits of paper, pens, envelopes, folders and other bits of stationery that, while only small, together add up to a lot of used energy, raw materials and potential waste. To reduce the environmental impact of these things, use eco-stationery. There are lots of firms selling things like recycled paper, pens made from recycled objects, such as old CD cases, biodegradable folders and marker pens that use non-toxic inks. One such firm is the Green Stationery Company (**www.greenstat.co.uk**), but there are lots more.

BUY RECYCLED FURNITURE Save all the energy and materials used in the process of making furniture by buying recycled items from outlets such as Recycled Business Furniture (**www.recycledbusinessfurniture.co.uk**). If you're a charity, school, community group or a start-up business, you can buy recycled office furniture at an even lower cost from charities such as Green Works (**www.green-works.co.uk**).

WOOD YOU BELIEVE IT? It is often said that forests are the lungs of the Earth, absorbing carbon dioxide and turning it into oxygen. The world's forests are also home to two-thirds of all land plant and animal species. But look around your office or workplace and the chances are you will see furniture made from illegal wood. Friends of the Earth estimates that 60% of the UK's tropical timber imports are illegally sourced from protected forests in places like Indonesia and Brazil. Apart from speeding up global warming, the practice threatens to wipe out species such as the tiger and orang-utan, and endangers the survival of indigenous tribes whose land is seized by criminal logging gangs. To make sure your furniture is made from ethically maintained and sustainable forests, check that it is certified by the Forest Stewardship Council (FSC). Blue Line (**www.blueline.uk.com**), for example, uses only FSC-certified timber in its range of office furniture.

AVOID BROMINATED FLAME RETARDANTS Brominated flame retardants (BFRs) are a group of chemicals used in fabrics, computers and plastics to counteract the spread of fires. They contribute to air pollution and are released into the environment both at the source of manufacture and through the everyday wear and tear of products. Disturbingly, scientists in Sweden have even discovered high levels of BFRs in the eggs of peregrine falcons on cliffs in Lapland, thousands of miles from the sources of their release. Several BFRs are proven hormone disrupters, interfering with the daily functioning of the body, and they can also disrupt the thyroid hormone and contaminate human breast milk. In fact, they're so bad that some countries have banned them altogether, and some major furniture suppliers, such as IKEA, have stopped using them. Always check a company's policy on BFRs when you buy new furniture.

TURN YOUR OFFICE GREEN We talked about putting a plant on your desk in chapter 3, but to really give your office a lift, landscape it with lots of CO_2 and toxin-absorbing plants. Some plants are better than others at absorbing the harmful toxins given off by things like office carpets, furniture and printers, and a good way to get the right balance is to call in the experts, such as Office Planters (**www.officeplants.co.uk**). As well as absorbing chemicals, plants can increase the humidity of dry offices. They have also been credited with reducing stress and helping to aid concentration.

Kitchens and bathrooms

LOOK AFTER YOUR FRIDGE Most offices have a fridge somewhere, buzzing quietly away, day and night. Fridges are one of the most energy-hungry electrical appliances, but there are lots of things you can do to diminish their appetite:

1. Keep the temperature between 3°C and 5°C – keeping a fridge below 3°C is unnecessary and wastes energy.

2. Keep coils free from dust – when dust gathers on the condenser coils at the back of your fridge, energy consumption can rise by 30%.

3. Buy a fridge saver plug – you can save 20% of your fridge's running costs by fitting one of these devices, which cut power to the fridge's motor when it doesn't need it. Buy a SavaPlug from Doctor Energy (www.doctorenergy.co.uk).

4. Free stand your fridge – keep it away from cookers or boilers and in a cool environment if possible.

5. Buy an A grade fridge – fridges are graded A to G according to their energy efficiency, so if you're buying a new one for the office, go for an A grade. If your boss doesn't want to stump up the extra cash, tell him he's likely to save the money back in the form of reduced electricity bills within 18 months.

GREEN SNACK MACHINE

Most company vending machines are full of unhealthy snacks produced by food and drink companies with less-than-perfect environmental records. They have already been banned in schools, so

isn't it time we grown-ups wised up, too? Rather than settle for the usual line-up, swap your vending machine for something more interesting, like one that sells Fairtrade or organic products, such as a snack machine from **www.fairtradevending.co.uk**.

TOP TIP – IFAW (INTERNATIONAL FUND FOR ANIMAL WELFARE) USE ORGANIC COTTON BAGS

Instead of using plastic bags when shopping for office supplies or kitchen essentials, switch to an organic cotton bag. Many fold up really easily and can be popped into a pocket or handbag and used as and when you need to transport lots of groceries or your lunch. Leave a supply by the office door so that your colleagues can pick them up as they head out to the shops. At IFAW we have produced a selection of these, which we give out to supporters and encourage staff to use for their shopping.

TOP TIP – ETHICAL CONSUMER MAGAZINE GET OFF THE BOTTLE

Get your company to sack the water cooler. Bottled water is damaging for a whole host of reasons. Extracting mineral water leads to water shortages, while transporting it contributes to climate change. Instead of shelling out for mineral water in a cooler, get your office to buy a plumbed-in water cooler instead. Alternatively, buy a terracotta water purifier, available from the Natural Collection (**www.naturalcollection. com**). This filters the water for you and doesn't require any electricity to keep it cool.

BECOME AN ECO-CUBIST Urinals in the men's toilets can be incredibly wasteful in their use of water. While some have a manual flush, most are set to flush automatically every few minutes. A typical urinal will flush 151,000 litres of water a year, costing an average of between £450 and £500. An extremely easy, eco-solution is to use something called eco-cubes (**www.eco-works.co.uk**). You simply place these cubes – which are made up of billions of natural, organic microbes – in each urinal and turn off the water at the urinal tap, saving you 100% water usage for each one. The eco-cubes slowly release the microbes down into the waste pipes, where they digest lime scale and uric scale and get rid of bad smells.

BUM DEAL FOR TREES I remember a long time ago, before recycling became a mainstream activity, someone asked me if I would use recycled toilet paper. The answer the questioner was getting from most people was a turned up nose and a firm 'no'. Of course, we all now know that recycled toilet paper is not made from used loo roll, but is a perfectly high-quality product. In the UK we use 2.85 billion rolls of toilet paper every year. If this were all recycled toilet paper, hundreds of thousands of trees would be saved. At the very least, your loo roll should be made from wood from sustainable forests, certified by the Forest Stewardship Council (FSC).

TAKE A ZERO-TOLERANCE APPROACH You could take your loo roll policy one step further, of course. Some of the bigger brands (such as Nouvelle and Kimberly Clark) may sell recycled products, but the greenest option is to source your toilet paper from a company that does not use virgin paper in any of its ranges, such as the Natural Collection, Traidcraft, Ecotopia, Essential and Suma brands.

HAND DRYERS VS PAPER TOWELS This thorny issue is guaranteed to keep environmentalists debating long into the night without a conclusive verdict being reached. Most studies that have been conducted favour hand dryers, but the results vary depending on the number of towels you suppose a person uses, or the length of time hands are left under a dryer. A dryer uses electricity to heat and blow air, while paper towels require energy to produce and are then either thrown away into landfill or recycled, which uses up yet more energy. If you do opt for dryers, the most energy efficient model is the Xlerator (**www.exceldryer. com**), which claims to use 80% less energy than standard dryers to dry hands in a third of the time.

Group hug

 TOP TIP – GLOBAL ACTION PLAN

ALTOGETHER NOW

Well done, you are making great green strides at work. You've cut down on paper use, you turn off your monitor when you are away from your desk, and you recycle your waste, and so on. But one of the greatest changes you can make in the office is to get others onboard. So encourage your colleagues to make a difference in the workplace if you notice that they could do something slightly differently to reduce its environmental footprint.

We tend to remember:
- 10% of what we read
- 20% of what we hear
- 30% of what we see
- 50% of what we read, hear and see
- 70% of what we say
- 90% of what we both say and do

The more colleagues you get to 'walk the talk', the more other people will join in as it is increasingly seen to be the norm.

 TOP TIP – FRIENDS OF THE EARTH

START A GREEN BEHAVIOUR TEAM

Friends of the Earth agrees. It recommends setting up an internal 'green team' to start changing people's behaviour using the following eight steps:

1. Select your project team (usually three to five people depending on the size of the organisation).

2. Agree on a specific and realistic focus for the group.

3. Get management buy-in.

4. Launch the initiative – inform people who you are and what you are doing, perhaps via an office quiz or at a staff meeting.

5. Start your first green action – put posters with green rules and tips around the building or next to printers.

6. Keep staff updated on a regular basis, using a staff newsletter or the intranet.

7. Build on your success – launch additional green actions to help build momentum.

8. Remember to have fun – change is possible, if you know how.

CASE STUDY
DEVON AND CORNWALL HOUSING ASSOCIATION

Devon and Cornwall Housing Association (DCHA) dedicated its staff conference this year to the environment. It asked every staff team to come up with two ideas it could implement to make the organisation greener, and it pinned these up around the venue. Community partners were invited to attend the conference and put up stalls, including those who could talk to staff about being green at home. Rose Hunter, DCHA's sustainable living coordinator, says that generally people who are environmentally conscious at home are keener to be green at work. To round the conference off, the organisation ran a *Who Wants To Be A Millionaire?* quiz based on its own environmental performance – with questions on things such as how much paper it uses every year. As a result of the conference, being environmentally responsible is now one of the DCHA's four key aims.

What a waste

The UK produces 434 million tonnes of waste every year
– that's enough to fill London's Albert Hall every two hours.
While the bulk of this is agricultural, mining, construction
and industrial waste, commercial office waste still accounts
for over 26 million tonnes a year. That's a lot of ink cartridges,
CDs, paper clips and leftover sandwiches. Any business
looking to improve its environmental credentials needs to
tackle the problem of waste. From the work kitchens and
bathrooms, to the typical workstation, there are opportunities
to reduce, reuse and recycle everywhere, if you know how
to spot them. And the good news is that it could save your
company money. So, what are you waiting for?

Waste policy

DO A WASTE AUDIT Before you start thinking about how to manage your waste, you should carry out a waste audit to find out where you are. Measure the types and amounts of waste produced in your workplace and use this as a starting point for gauging the level of improvement any waste minimisation programme achieves. Your waste audit should:

1. Identify all points at which waste is generated.
2. Identify the origin of each type of waste.
3. Measure the quantity of each type of waste, and its environmental impact.
4. Establish a method for the continued monitoring of waste levels.
5. Identify the current costs of dealing with waste.
6. Look at opportunities to reduce, recycle or reuse the waste.
7. Set waste minimisation targets.
8. Communicate the results of your audit to the rest of your company.

GET AN EXPERT WASTE APPRAISAL The government-funded organisation Envirowise can arrange for an independent expert to visit your workplace free of charge to assess your waste management policy and practices for you. It will then offer tailored guidance to help you reduce waste and save money. Visit **www.envirowise.gov.uk**.

COMMUNICATE YOUR POLICY TO STAFF Without your colleagues on board, achieving waste minimisation in some areas will be impossible. Make sure everyone knows about policies to reduce waste through your intranet, newsletter or noticeboard. Make sure staff know who to approach if they have questions. And try to think up some relevant incentives, such as a donation to a charity chosen by staff from the money saved by reducing waste.

CASE STUDY
INTERFACE

US carpet producer Interface first began tackling waste in 1995. It began its waste minimisation plan by consulting its staff, establishing an initiative called QUEST (Quality Using Employee Suggestions and Teamwork) to ensure that all processes throughout the business took waste reduction into account. The company looked beyond its own production procedures, requesting that all suppliers minimise their packaging and, where possible, the company made efforts to reclaim packaging from customers for on-site recycling. Since 1995, Interface's waste initiatives have saved it a total of US$336 million and reduced the amount of waste it sends to landfill by 65%.

COLLECT PRNS, IF YOU HAVE TO If your company has a turnover in excess of £2 million and you handle large amounts of packaging (over 50 tonnes a year) either as a manufacturer, packager or seller of goods, you are legally obliged to take responsibility for the amount of waste you send to landfill sites. For every tonne of packaging you recover for reuse or recycling, you get a certain number of Package Recovery Notes (PRNs) which have a variable market value, and you have a set target for the number of PRNs you are obliged to amass over the year. If all this sounds hellishly complicated, you can pay a compliance scheme to recover your targeted waste for you, such as PRN Brokers (**www.prnbrokers.co.uk**). For more details on PRNs, contact NetRegs (**www.netregs.gov.uk**).

TOP TIP – ETHICAL CONSUMER MAGAZINE
CHAMPIONSHIP MANAGER

Instigate a waste-minimisation manager and then create a waste minimisation championship! Create a league table to incentivise green behaviour among staff, with rewards for the greenest member!

Reduce

MINIMISE **Virtually every solution put forward to combat global warming has the fatal flaw that it still requires the use of energy at some stage in its production, from recycling to biofuels. The only faultless solution in purely environmental terms is to produce less and consume less. This is generally bad news for businesses, except when it comes to waste. Here, the environmental and commercial messages walk hand in hand. Businesses typically spend 4.5% of their turnover on waste disposal. The equation is simple: reduce waste and you will save money and help protect the environment.**

CUT DOWN DELIVERY WASTE Whatever your business, you are likely to receive deliveries of some packaged items. Put pressure on your suppliers to reduce the amount of packaging and to put things in reusable packaging where possible. For example, plastic boxes that suppliers can take back and reuse again and again could be used instead or cardboard boxes.

USE LESS PACKAGING ON YOUR PRODUCTS Excessive packaging on your products may look nice, but it is environmentally wasteful. Not only does it require energy to produce, but it then needs to be disposed of, usually ending up in landfill. Consumers are forever being encouraged to buy products with less packaging, so the commercial value of fancy disposable boxes and cases is slowly diminishing. Indeed, a MORI survey in 2007 found that 92% of supermarket shoppers wished to see a reduction in the overall amount of packaging.

MAKE THINGS LAST LONGER For every tonne of waste at the user's end of a manufactured item, there are, on average, five tonnes of waste at the manufacturing stage and 20 tonnes at the initial resource extraction stage. So, when you throw something away, even a pen, it may seem small and insignificant, but the accumulated waste is huge. Buying a replacement means creating all that waste again. Of course, an office with ageing computers and pens that barely work will not be as productive, but think twice before upgrading equipment and try to find the optimum balance in terms of the lifecycle of things. Getting this balance right will save you money in terms of reducing waste and in reducing purchasing costs.

WATER Treating and pumping water to your office requires huge amounts of electricity, so cutting out waste will save energy, and will also save you money. If every business in the east of England left just one tap dripping for just one day, it would lead to 5.2 million litres of water being wasted, and cost businesses in the region more than £400,000. The government-run agency Envirowise will provide a free audit of how much water your business uses and advise you on how to reduce wastage as part of its Big Splash campaign. Visit **www.envirowise.gov.uk/bigsplash**.

TOP TIP – NATURAL COLLECTION
SUSTAINABLE STAPLING
Making a green statement can speak volumes about your commitment to both the planet and the corporate bottom line. So who would have thought that the simple stapler could be such a powerful symbol? The stapleless stapler uses punch folding to avoid the need for staples, clipping up to four pages together and saving metal and energy at the same time. Visit **www.naturalcollection.com**.

Reuse

REUSE STUFF **While recycling is good, reusing is better. Try to avoid throwing away things you can easily reuse, such as pieces of paper, envelopes or paper clips. As much as possible, only use a new or disposable product when there's no reusable alternative available. If each of the UK's**

10 million office workers used just one less staple a day by reusing a paper clip, it could save an incredible 120 tonnes of steel each year.

REUSE ENVELOPES Envelopes are easy to reuse, saving paper and reducing the need to recycle. For internal use you can just cross out the old address and write in the new one. To reuse envelopes externally, you can buy address labels from charities such as Friends of the Earth (**www.foe.co.uk**), which you stick over the old name and address saving resources and promoting the causes of the charity at the same time.

TOP TIP – COMMUNITY REPAINT
DONATE LEFTOVER PAINT

Each year approximately 80 million litres of paint are bought in the UK and not used; left stored in stockrooms or garages or just thrown away. That's enough paint to fill 33 Olympic-sized swimming pools. So, instead of sending your paint to landfill, donate it to Community RePaint. The UK-wide network of 70 community-based organisations collects leftover, reusable paint from businesses, the public, retailers, decorators and the paint trade, and then passes it on to local charities, voluntary organisations and community groups for redecoration projects. To find your nearest donation point, visit **www.communityrepaint.org.uk**.

FOOD According to wasteonline.org.uk, food actually accounts for the biggest chunk of office and commercial waste. If you are in the catering industry, or your workplace has a staff canteen or café, make sure any still edible waste is given to the charity Fareshare (**www.fareshare.org.uk**), which will distribute it to those who cannot afford a healthy meal. Fareshare contributes to 3.3 million meals to 12,000 people across the UK. Any food it doesn't distribute, it uses as compost or animal feed.

THINK OUTSIDE THE BOX Try to think creatively about how you can reuse waste objects in your everyday business. The band Recoup (**www.myspace.com/recoup**), for example, used old crisp packets turned inside out for the cover of their latest CD. The band said that the reason it chose crisp packets was because they are hard to recycle, they are durable, the perfect shape for a CD and when turned inside out they are all uniform silver in colour.

Recycle

DON'T BIN IT, RECYCLE IT **Despite your best efforts, some things just can't be reused and need to be thrown away. The next challenge is to prolong the life of the raw materials used in a product by recycling it. Recycling not only reduces the burden on landfill, it also saves energy. It takes 70% less energy to recycle paper, for example, than it does to make it from raw materials.**

COMPUTERS With the speed of technological change and the need to keep up to date in order to remain competitive, business computers become obsolete very quickly. British industry throws out a staggering one million computers every year, usually because they won't run the latest software. Until recently, most of these still-working computers – made up of many toxins and heavy metals – ended up in landfill sites or being shipped out to the developing world where they were dismantled by unprotected migrant workers. However, in 2007 the Waste Electrical and Electronic Equipment (WEEE) directive came into force making retailers responsible for recycling computers. So, when you buy a new set of laptops, for example, the firm you buy them from should take back your old ones and recycle them – saving you from having to do anything, except make sure they do.

★ **TOP TIP – GREEN GUY (WWW.GREENGUY.CO.UK)**
GET YOUR OFFICE COMPOSTING
It's hard to believe that old tea bags, apple cores and banana skins add up to

a lot of office rubbish, but they actually make up a massive amount of our working waste. Why should we be bothered? Well, lots of organic waste in landfill equals lots of greenhouse gases. If you work for a big company, lobby your environmental or facilities manager to arrange for food waste bins and collections to be taken away for large-scale composting. If you're at a smaller business, just get a Bokashi composter from the likes of Wiggly Wigglers (**www.wigglywigglers.co.uk**) and put one in the kitchen.

CONNECT WITH THE WASTE COLLECTORS So, you have all the right intentions and you want to recycle everything, but you can't find a local recycling company to take your waste. Fear thee not, Waste Connect (**www.wasteconnect.co.uk**) has a helpline you can call: 0905 535 0940.

CASE STUDY
MCDONALD'S

OK, McDonald's may be an odd choice for an example of good environmental practice, but if McDonald's is taking climate change seriously then so should you. In Sweden, McDonald's was embarrassed by public demonstrations over its packaging, so it implemented a waste audit. As well as recommending a change to compostable packaging, the audit found that 35% of the company's waste was actually liquid – unfinished drinks and ice. So, it put a sink next to the bins and put up a sign asking customers to empty their drinks. It then went further and began sorting all of its waste and recycling it, to the extent that in Sweden, at least, McDonald's now recycles 97% of its waste, and its restaurants send on average just one bag of unsorted waste to landfill each month.

GIVE YOUR COMPUTERS TO CHARITY While recycling computers is better than sending them to fester on a landfill site, it still seems a bit wasteful to dismantle a fully-functioning machine for its component parts. A better option is to give it to one of the many charities that have been set up to take old but working computers from businesses and distribute them to those who can't afford to buy them new, both in the UK and in the developing world. For a full list of charities and companies that reuse old computers and other computer equipment, visit **www.itforcharities.co.uk**.

USE YOUR KITCHEN OIL TO MAKE BIOFUEL While biofuel has received lots of negative attention from environmentalists recently (see The Commute chapter), this is centred on the problems of growing crops specifically for biofuel. There is no argument against reusing waste cooking oil to make biofuel. If your workplace has a kitchen with a deep fryer, learn how to turn its waste oil into biofuel (the website **www.biodieselcommunity.org** has instructions). If you don't have a vehicle to put it in, you may be able to sell it locally to other biofuel users. At the risk of promoting McDonald's too much, it recently announced that it was going to run all of its lorries in the UK on biofuel produced from the waste oil from its restaurants, which can only be seen as a commendable move.

MOBILE PHONES Mobile phone companies have convinced us of the need to upgrade our phones regularly, even though the old ones work perfectly well. As a result, there are approximately 25 million phones lying dormant in the UK. That's 2,500 tonnes of waste, the equivalent of 14 Jumbo jets. Instead of binning your old mobile phones, or leaving them in a drawer somewhere creating a potential problem for the future, recycle them. There are many schemes collecting old phones and sending them out to developing countries, where often there is no landline infrastructure and people rely on mobile phones. These can, however, be expensive to buy new. Corporate Mobile Recycling (**www.cmrecycling.co.uk**) is a scheme set up in partnership with Oxfam with business users in mind and offers you the chance to make money from your old phones – or for additional ethical kudos you can donate your gains to charity through the scheme.

DON'T JUST USE YOUR LOCAL FACILITIES Businesses are not legally allowed to use recycling sites set up for domestic use, such as bottle banks and local skips. If you want to recycle, contact your local council and speak to the recycling officer or approach a waste management company (such as the Waste Recycling Group – **www.wrg.co.uk**) to arrange for it to be collected. There will be a fee for this, but it should be cheaper than getting your non-recycled waste collected.

RECYCLE YOUR CDS CDs are used with almost the same abandon as paper in some offices – you probably have a pile of them on your desk or in your drawer. Don't throw them away. CDs are 100% recyclable – even the cases. Instead, send them to a recycling firm, such as Polymer Recycling (**www.polymerrecycling.co.uk**), which will turn them into things like burglar alarms and car reflectors.

USE REWRITEABLE CDS AND DVDS Some CDs you can use only once, called CD-Rs, and some you can use again and again, called CD-RWs. No prizes for guessing which are the most environmentally friendly. If you need to store lots of information, such as large video files, use a DVD instead, as you'll fit more on a disk that uses a comparable amount of energy to produce and package.

FIND ANOTHER USE FOR CDS Old CDs can be used in numerous ways – artists may use them to make sculptures (see George Radebaugh's work at **www.cdsculpture.com**), gardeners can use them to scare birds away, or you can use them as coasters for your coffee. For more ideas, the website **www.hintsandthings.co.uk** has compiled a list of 101 things to do with old CDs. You could even use one to stop your boss creeping up behind you by sticking it on the corner of your computer screen like a rear-view mirror.

RECYCLE GLASS BOTTLES After an office celebration, or a corporate event involving lots of bottles of wine, make sure any glass is recycled and not dumped in the bin. Recycling just one glass bottle saves enough energy to power a TV set for an hour and a half, while for every tonne of glass recycled, 135 litres of oil and 1.2 tonnes of ash, sand and limestone are saved.

PLASTIC BOTTLES Plastic bottles should also be recycled. By recycling one plastic bottle you can conserve enough energy to light a 60W light bulb for three hours. Put recycling facilities in the office for those who drink water and other soft drinks from plastic bottles.

PLASTIC CUPS If you choose to use plastic cups for drinking water or coffee (see Office Politics chapter), recycle them. This is free, providing you sign up to the save-a-cup scheme (**www.save-a-cup.co.uk**). The scheme, run by the catering and vending industry, turns hard-walled polystyrene cups into things such as pens, key rings and coasters. The scheme is in some ways an attempt to mitigate criticism of the use of plastic cups in the workplace and so some environmentalists would argue that by supporting the scheme you are encouraging the continued use of plastic cups. As we mentioned earlier, this is hard to quantify, but whatever you do, don't simply use them and throw them in the bin.

Printing practice

STOP PRINTING GOBBLEDEGOOK We all know it happens. You print out a document, or a webpage, and at the end the printer spews out an extra blank page or one with some useless jargon from the bottom of an email. All this wasted paper (and ink) adds up – the average office worker uses 50 sheets of paper a day – so when you print something out, use the print preview option to check your document doesn't have any blank pages attached. Only print out the pages you need. And if a webpage has a 'printer-friendly' version (some do), use it. If all this is too technical for you, GreenPrint is a piece of software that will analyse your document for you when you click 'print', identify any unwanted or wasted pages, and then make sure your printer doesn't print them. It will even keep a track of how much waste you have avoided and calculate how much money this has saved you. Visit www.printgreener.com.

TWO FOR THE PRICE OF ONE You can also save paper by printing and photocopying on both sides of each page – your machine may refer to this as 'duplex' printing. Not all printers have the option to do this automatically, but most copiers do. Think of all the extra trees that would have to be cut down, transported and processed (a lot), if books and newspapers were only printed on one side of each page. So why should office documents be any different?

DO NOT PRINT THIS TIP Another way to cut down on wasteful printing is to get your IT department to put a message at the end of every staff email saying 'Please don't print this email', or something like that. You could add some environmental fact, to back up the sentiment, such as the fact that 5 million tonnes of printing and writing paper are thrown away by UK businesses each year. If your company is against the idea of attaching such a message to every email, you can add it to your own emails in most mail systems, such as Outlook, through the Add Signature option (in Outlook, go to Tools, then Options and then click on the Signature tab).

USE RECYCLED PAPER... Recycling waste paper is the beginning of the recycling circle. Buying and using recycled paper is the last stage, and without people using recycled products, recycling won't work. So, for all those print jobs that you do have to do, try to get your company to order chlorine-free recycled paper (such as **www.evolve-papers.com**). Using recycled paper saves energy and means less carbon-absorbing trees have to be cut down and fewer wildlife habitats need to be destroyed. Also, go for a paper free of chlorine bleaches, which produce dioxins that can, when they find their way into the water system, be harmful to animals and humans.

... AND VEGETABLE INK It is not only the paper you need to worry about. The inks used in many printers can be very damaging to the environment. If you can, go for vegetable- or water-based inks. Many of the chemicals in standard inks, known ominously as Volatile Organic Compounds (VOCs), not only contribute to the depletion of the ozone layer, but can cause health problems for staff. According to the US Environmental Protection Agency, standard office inks can cause eye, nose and throat irritation, headaches, loss of coordination, nausea, and can even damage your liver, kidney and central nervous system. Although the most severe of these problems are unlikely to afflict the average office with a few small printers, large printing firms should be particularly careful about using them. Toxic metals are also commonly found in many standard inks, and they too can cause health and environmental problems.

INK CARTRIDGES When your printer cartridge runs out of ink, don't just throw it in the bin. Laser cartridges can be taken apart and remanufactured for around a third of the price of a new cartridge, saving a litre of oil and reducing landfill. Inkjet cartridges, meanwhile, can be given to companies and charities who will clean them, refill them and sell them on – again saving the energy of producing new cartridges and reducing landfill. ActionAid Recycling (**www.actionaidrecycling.org.uk**), for example, will give you a cartridge collection box to put in your office and freepost envelopes so that you can send collected cartridges off for recycling. For a list of other recycling companies specialising in printer cartridges, visit the UK Cartridge Remanufacturers Association at **www.ukcra.com**.

USE REFILLABLE CARTRIDGES Save cartridge waste altogether by using refillable cartridges. There is a fierce ongoing debate over the quality of refilled ink cartridges between printer manufacturers who sell non-refillable cartridges and those that sell refillable inks – with some even claiming the refilled cartridges are better than the originals. As well as being more eco-friendly, refills are much cheaper. Refilling the cartridges can be messy, however, so it is best to get it done by professionals – such as the people who sold them to you in the first place. Also, avoid refill cartridges that claim to fit a large range of printers, as they are more likely to produce poor-quality results.

USE HEMP PAPER If you're not using recycled paper, you should consider using hemp paper. Hemp produces up to four times more pulp per acre than timber and produces higher-quality paper. It recycles more times than wood pulp and there are no environmentally damaging bleaching processes involved in its production. And unlike other fibre crops, it doesn't need the intensive use of herbicides and pesticides to grow. However, its association with cannabis has long been hemp's Achilles' heel, and although commercial hemp growing has occurred in the UK since 1993, the government has been unwilling to support hemp farmers. If you are, however, visit the Hemp Shop's website at **www.thehempshop.co.uk**.

PUT A RECYCLING BIN BESIDE THE PRINTER AND PHOTOCOPIER This one sounds obvious, but strategic placement of recycling bins will make a difference. Only the most conscientious workers will seek out a recycling bin if there isn't one nearby.

Batteries

RUNNING ON EMPTY Batteries are everywhere: in our phones, laptops, cars, iPods and watches. Yet, according to the charity Waste Watch (www.wasteonline.org.uk), less than 2% of batteries in the UK are recycled. This is despite the fact that they contain potentially toxic heavy metals such as cadmium and mercury which, when disposed of in landfill sites, seep into the ground and rivers. These not only endanger wildlife, but can also reach the human food chain through fish. So, when a battery dies, recycle it. If your local council won't collect it, a recycling firm like Rabbitt (www.worktwice.co.uk/rabbitt) will. Rabbitt will even provide you with a battery-shaped recycling box for your workplace.

GO FOR LONGER LIFE Of course, the way you use an electronic device will determine how long the battery will last before you need to recharge it, or recycle it and get another one. For example, watching DVDs on your laptop will use up more juice than writing an email. Good battery care can also prolong shelf life. For tips and advice on looking after your batteries, take a trip to BatteryUniversity.com (**www.batteryuniversity.com**).

IT'S A WIND-UP Even better than recycling batteries is to avoid using them altogether by getting yourself a wind-up device. You may struggle to find a wind-up laptop, but you can get arm-powered radios, torches and even mobile-phone chargers. Not only are they extremely eco-friendly and cheap, they provide good exercise, too. For the ultimate wind-up device, the inventor of the first wind-up radio, Trevor Baylis, has brought out an Eco Media Player (available from **www.ethicalsuperstore.com**), which plays music and videos, and functions as a torch, a sound recorder, photo viewer, phone charger and data storage device.

RECHARGE OF THE LIGHT BRIGADE Use rechargeable batteries where you can. According to Waste Watch, the energy required to manufacture a battery is 50 times greater than the energy it gives out – so that's a lot of waste you'll be saving. It also means less contamination from toxic metals seeping into the earth.

WATER POWER Japanese inventor Susumu Suzuki only revealed his water-powered batteries to the world at the end of 2006, but already the market is full of gadgets that run on them. One of the best is the desk clock from Nigel's Eco Store (**www.nigelsecostore.com**). When they run out, the batteries just need to be refilled with a little water and they're ready to go again. No toxic heavy metals required.

BACK FROM THE DEAD Most dead batteries still have life in them. You may remember when you were at school the classroom know-it-all taking a dead battery, shaking it vigorously and then placing it back in a device and it miraculously working again. Well, while shaking batteries can bring limited success, a device called a battery regenerator can restore batteries back to 95% of their original power and can be used on the same battery up to 100 times. So don't throw away those dead batteries until they really are dead. Battery refreshers can be bought from Doctor Energy (**www.doctorenergy.co.uk**).

Business class

Air travel may only account for 2% of the world's CO_2 emissions, but as the fastest-rising contributor it is the bulls-eye target for many environmental campaigners. Any eco-conscious business traveller who had to pass the Climate Camp protesters surrounding Heathrow Airport in the summer of 2007 would have boarded the plane with a pang of guilt. But business will go on, and it will involve travel. Even if you can bring yourself to skip on that conference in the Bahamas, you and your colleagues still have to get to work and back each day. There are still clients to see, meetings to attend. As with everything, there are nearly always greener options. The trick is getting as many of your colleagues as you can to use them.

Day to day travel

TAXI DRIVER While your green conscience may hark after cleaner, alternative forms of transport, there are times when the speed and convenience of a taxi is what is required. But if you do have to call a cab, at least make it a green one. A number of firms, such as London's Go Green Car (www.gogreencar.co.uk) now run fleets of hybrid cars. These save fuel and hence emissions by employing an electric motor to help the regular petrol motor when accelerating. London's Radio Taxis (www.radiotaxis.co.uk) has gone even further and developed its own biofuel blend, made with UK-grown oil-seed rape, to run its fleet of black cabs, which it says results in 7% less CO_2 emissions.
If you can't find a green taxi firm in your area, maybe you can put pressure on your local cabbies to clean up their act. The incentive of a business account may be all it takes.

TOP TIP – CARPLUS
CAR SHARING

Carplus (**www.carplus.org.uk**) says car sharing can form an important part of a company travel plan by matching together staff making similar journeys either in to work or as part of their job. This can be done with the aid of a computer program, a straightforward spreadsheet or simply by using a noticeboard. Car sharing provides huge financial benefits for staff, cutting travel costs in half when two people share. In addition, any carbon emissions are reduced by 50% and car sharers are doing their bit to reduce congestion, both on the journey to work and in the car park.

TAKE PART IN NATIONAL LIFTSHARE DAY Encourage lift sharing among your colleagues by taking part in National Liftshare Day (**www.nationalliftshareday.org**). If there's no one going your way on National Liftshare Day, you can find a travelling companion on the website **www.liftshare.com**. Typical regular *lift*share members, it says, save around £1,000 and one tonne of CO_2 each year by sharing their daily journey.

CASE STUDY
CULHAM SCIENCE CENTRE

Culham Science Centre in Abingdon, Oxfordshire, has got into car sharing in a big way. It began by taking part in National Liftshare Day in 2006. As an incentive, anyone arriving to work in a shared car that day was entered into a prize draw for a £50 gardening voucher (a nice green incentive). The organisers recorded the number of car sharers on the day and set themselves the target of increasing that number before the next National Liftshare Day. This target spurred them on to team up with *lift*share who helped them set up their own website, **www.culhamcarshare.com**, which their staff and other users in the area use to team up and share journeys. Anyone registering in the first month was entered into a prize draw for a mountain bike (the incentives were getting bigger!). By 2007, the site had generated 87 new users and saved an estimated five tonnes of CO_2 emissions.

DITCH CARS COMPLETELY FOR A DAY Go one step further than lift sharing and get your colleagues to leave their cars at home altogether on European Car Free Day, also known as In Town Without My Car Day. In 2006, 1,300 towns and cities in 40 countries took part in the campaign, closing off streets to traffic. Find out if your town is involved by visiting the website at **www.dft.gov.uk/itwmc**. If nothing is happening in your area, why not take the local lead and get things started?

NATIONAL BIKE TO WORK WEEK Here's another excuse to get your colleagues out of their cars: National Bike to Work Week. It takes place every June and, as the name suggests, it encourages people to cycle to work instead of drive. Details can be found at **www.bikeweek.org.uk**.

CASE STUDY
SANDWELL HOSPITAL

The Sandwell Hospital in Birmingham conducted a survey among its 3,000 staff and found that only 10 regularly cycled to work. The hospital's chief executive decided to tackle this by giving £15,000 to a member of staff anointed as the hospital's 'cycle champion'. In addition to this, 20 bikes were donated by Dawes cycle shop and the hospital purchased 30 Brompton folding bikes, which staff were able to borrow or buy at a discount. With the £15,000, the cycle champion created a secure storage facility for bikes, complete with clothes-drying facilities, and by the end of the year there were already 40 staff regularly cycling to work. To celebrate this result, a staff cycling holiday in Cornwall was arranged. This proved a great success, with people taking up cycling to work in order to get fit enough for the holiday. Participants on the trip were even given an extra day's holiday from work. To counter any objections, this was positioned as a reward in recognition of the fact that cyclists generally take fewer days off due to illness.

TOP TIP – WWW.GREENSHOP.CO.UK
CYCLESCHEME

Ask your employer to join Cyclescheme (**www.cyclescheme.co.uk**). This government scheme has been set up to encourage both employers and employees to make the most of the Green Transport Plan. It takes advantage of unique tax benefits, so you can save up to 50% on the price of a new bike. It works like this:

1. Employer joins scheme.

2. Employee goes to approved bike shop and chooses bike.

3. Employee reports back to boss who arranges payment.

4. Transaction is approved by Cyclescheme and a voucher is arranged.

5. Employee then returns to bike shop and collects bike.

6. Employee now pays for bike in instalments through pay packet, taken pre-tax and over an agreed period.

Brilliant!

FIND A BIKE BUDDY Smooth the transition from driving to cycling by teaming up nervous beginners with experienced 'bike buddies' who live in the same area, can show them the best routes home and answer any other bike-related queries they may have.

GET A FREE BREAKFAST The government has set up a scheme to enable employers to provide staff who cycle to work with six free breakfasts a year. Get your company to take advantage of the scheme, and use them on bike promotion days, such as the aforementioned National Bike to Work Week, to give these days maximum appeal. Visit **www.ctc.org.uk**.

PUT A BUG IN THE SYSTEM Set up a bicycle user group, or BUG, in your office. A BUG is a loose association of bike users and it works within the company to improve conditions for cyclists, share ideas and promote cycling to other staff. Here are a few examples of things BUGs can get up to:

1. Produce a regular newsletter.

2. Set up a BUG website or intranet site.

3. Organise bike doctor visits.

4. Arrange lunchtime talks or presentations about cycling.

5. Run a cyclists' information service supplying free maps, leaflets and other advice.

6. Operate a 'bike buddy' scheme (see previous page).

7. Negotiate a staff discount from a local bike shop.

SPREAD THE WORD Use whatever means possible to let your colleagues know about greener ways to get to work. Provide accessible information about public transport, or maps with good cycle and walking routes. Use the intranet to spread the word further to offices on other sites, if you work for a large company.

AVOID UNNECESSARY MEETINGS Reduce travel needs by making use of technology. We talk about cutting down on meetings through video and audio conferencing in chapter 13, but even ancient technologies, such as email, can help reduce the need to travel. And if email is too slow, try instant messaging. Of course, there are times when face-to-face contact is important, but factor in the environmental cost when planning meetings, particularly if you travel by car, and if you can, avoid going anywhere.

SIGN YOUR COMPANY UP FOR A CORPORATE CHALLENGE

Corporate Challenge runs are basically competitive fun runs for businesses and other organisations. You enter a team, usually at least four people, and then you compete for a trophy in a race against other local organisations. Events like this are good for team building and for encouraging your colleagues to put on their running shoes, which may lead to people running to and from work instead of taking the car. It is also a chance to raise some money for charity. Corporate Challenge runs take place across the country, often within other races, such as city marathons and half-marathons.

BRING THE BANK TO YOUR OFFICE
Do people hop in their cars at lunchtime to pop to the bank or the dry-cleaners? If your office is large enough, you may be able to bring popular services in-house. Ask your staff which services they would use in the workplace and you may be able to find businesses willing to come to you and provide them. Even little things, such as selling stamps at reception, may help reduce travel needs if your workplace is in an isolated location.

Getting away

STAY ON THE GROUND We all know that one of the worst things an individual can do in terms of contributing to global warming is to take a flight. But did you know it may be even worse if you board a plane while on a business trip? This is because, according to Professor Peter James of the UK Centre for Environmental and Economic Development, airlines rely on business-class passengers, who generally pay more for their seats, to make flights profitable. Without business-class passengers, Professor James says, airlines would be forced to put up the prices of standard tickets, which would mean fewer people would fly and hence there would be fewer flights. Just another reason to stay grounded, if you can.

TAKE THE TRAIN Train journeys are as much as 75% more CO_2-efficient than the airline equivalent, so if you have a choice, take the train. Train journeys may also get you there more quickly than you expect. Ryanair was recently admonished by the Advertising Standards Authority for claiming its flight from London to Brussels was cheaper and faster than making the journey by Eurostar. However, when getting to and from airports – both of which are way outside the city centres – was factored in, the Ryanair trip was not only more expensive, but slower. For detailed information on train routes throughout Europe, visit **www.seat61.com**.

ON A LIGHTER PLANE You may get a funny look from the travel agent, but if you really do have to take a flight, ask what type of plane you'll be flying in. The new Boeing 787 Dreamliner, for example, is made from lightweight plastic, which makes it 20% more fuel efficient than similar-sized aircraft (it seats 330 passengers). Its specially treated engines also reduce noise emissions by as much as 60%. And if you are flying with budget airline Flybe, you will find an eco-label for the plane used on each flight when you book a ticket online, giving the plane an eco-rating from A to F, with A being the most ecologically sound – although the fact that most of its planes score an A or B hardly suggests the ratings should be taken with a pinch of salt.

TAKE DAYTIME FLIGHTS According to scientists at the University of Reading, flying at night or in the winter is more environmentally damaging than flying during the day. The reasons are complex, but basically, the cooler air at night or during the winter is more likely to produce condensation trails when the hot fumes from the plane are emitted. These trails trap the Earth's heat and create a 'greenhouse effect' that adds to the warming of the atmosphere. During the day, however, these trails can help reflect heat away from the Earth, creating a cooling effect. The researchers found that although night flights only account for only 25% of the daily air traffic, they contribute 60 to 80% of the warming caused by commercial flights. At the same time, winter flights account for only 22% of the annual number of commercial flights, but contribute half of the annual warming effect.

TAKE THE SILVERJET Another flying option, if you simply must take the plane, is the Silverjet. This business-only airline flies between London and New York and calls itself 'the world's first carbon-neutral airline'. This rather grand title is derived from the fact that carbon offsetting is offered to all passengers on its flights at the time of booking. As we mention in chapter 11, offsetting is not the miracle solution it is often said to be, but in most cases the projects funded are environmentally beneficial. You can offset your carbon independently, but on the Silverjet you have the satisfaction of knowing the whole flight is being offset if you opt to do so.

TAKE OUT ECO-FRIENDLY TRAVEL INSURANCE If your airline won't offset your carbon for you, then you can get travel insurance that does, such as the Climate Care insurance, which is offered in conjunction with Axa. Visit **www.climatesure.co.uk**.

USE THE EUROSTAR The Eurostar has just got quicker. Due to faster track being laid on the British leg of the journey, it can now travel from the centre of London to the centre of Paris in just over two hours. As a result, travel from the UK to many more parts of Europe will now not only be more eco-friendly, but also quicker by train. For more information, visit **www.eurostar.com**.

SHARE THE WORLD Just because you're travelling abroad doesn't mean you have to ditch your green morals and hire a high-powered sports car. Car sharing is a global practice, as you'll see from a quick glance at **www.carpoolworld.com**. If you're going to a corporate event, try to get the organisers to list it on the carpoolworld.com website and advertise it to other attendees. Then, instead of everyone hiring their own car, causing lots of unnecessary pollution, congestion and the rest, you can get together and give each other lifts. It may even turn out to be an invaluable networking tool.

HIRE A GREENER CAR If car sharing abroad is a bit daunting, you can still choose the greenest option when hiring a car. Some of the larger car-hire firms are now offering low-emission cars. Hertz, for example, offers slightly more efficient than average cars as part of its 'Green Collection' in 50 selected outlets across Europe. Failing that, choose the car with the smallest engine and go for diesel over petrol, as it's more fuel-efficient.

ALWAYS THINK LOCAL Many foreign destinations depend on tourism to survive, but often they find the bulk of the profits being siphoned off by multi-national companies running all-inclusive hotel complexes that sell goods imported from the visitors' own countries of origin. Try to support the local economy as much as possible by buying locally produced gifts, although be sure to avoid anything made from endangered animals, coral or plants. Also, try to eat in local restaurants and shop in local markets. In some places, haggling is common, but don't become obsessed with getting the cheapest price – remember how wealthy you are compared to local people in some countries.

LOOK FOR THE GREEN GLOBE SIGN Green Globe 21 is a global benchmarking programme for sustainable travel. Initiated by the World Travel and Tourism Council, it is based on Agenda 21 and the principles for sustainable development set out at the Rio Earth Summit in 1992. The programme gives certification to hotels, airlines and travel agents in more than 100 countries, all of which meet the necessary standards on social and environmental issues, from greenhouse gas emissions to noise control. Visit **www.greenglobe21.com**.

BY THE LIGHT OF THE SUN If you're heading somewhere hot and sunny, bring a solar charger with you. As well as being eco-friendly and useful when you're away from a wall socket, it also solves all those problems of finding plug adapters and dealing with electricity supplies in different voltages. The FreeLoader portable solar charger from Nigel's Eco Store (**www.nigelsecostore.com**), for example, will charge your phone, your BlackBerry®, your iPod, your digital camera and your sat nav. If you use all those gadgets think of all the emissions you'll be saving by powering them by the sun.

PUT IT IN A JUICE BAG Wherever you go, you'll always need to take a bag. Juice bags are briefcases, rucksacks and beach bags with in-built solar panels that sustainably charge all your electronic gadgets – although not your laptop, unfortunately – while on the road. Visit **www.rewarestore.com**.

TRAVEL LIGHT There is a reason airlines charge you extra if you bring too much baggage with you when you check in for a flight. The heavier your bags, the more fuel it will take to carry them. The more fuel used, the more emissions produced. If, for example, on an eight-hour flight, you checked in bags weighing 10kg instead of 20kg, you would be saving over four litres of aviation fuel. If everyone on your flight did the same, it would add up to a saving in CO_2 emissions of over two tonnes. This basic principle works for any form of transport you may take during your journey. So, try to avoid bringing the proverbial everything-but-the-kitchen-sink.

Hotels

NO CHANGE No matter how smart the hotel is that you choose to stay in, there is no real reason for it to change your sheets and towels every day as a matter of course. The largest chunk of a hotel's energy use – 42% – goes on heating water, much of which is used for doing huge piles of barely used laundry. If the hotel you're staying in doesn't already have a 'no change' policy, perhaps you should suggest it gets one. Or, at the very least, leave a note asking the chambermaids not to change the sheets and towels every day.

DON'T USE THE MINI FREEBIES They may be small, but they can have a big impact on the environment. The production of mini bottles and containers of soaps and shampoos is big business and uses significant amounts of energy. Hotels could save on thousands of bags of waste each year by using refillable dispensers for shampoo and skincare lotions, and by recycling soaps. If your hotel is using the mini versions, suggest it doesn't, or find another hotel.

FIND AN ECO-HOTEL An eco-hotel doesn't have to mean one with composting toilets and organic muesli for breakfast – although if that's what you are looking for, try the Hoopoe Yurt Hotel in Andalucia, Spain. The Green Business Tourism Scheme (**www.green-business. co.uk**) gives eco-conscious hotels in the UK bronze, silver and gold awards depending on just how green they are. The criteria covers everything from using local food and drink to putting up nesting boxes for birds. To find out about similar eco-labels for hotels in Europe, visit **www.visit21.net**.

GREEN HOTEL The Green Hotels Association is a group of hotels in the US that were asking their guests to consider reusing sheets and towels long before it became fashionable. For a full list of member hotels visit the website at **www.greenhotels.com**.

EAT GREEN One of the joys of travelling abroad is sampling the local cuisine, so try to order dishes made from local ingredients – it will help cut down on food miles. If you're in a country in which you can drink tap water safely, ask for that instead of bottled water.

CHECK YOUR HOTEL'S ETHICAL POLICY The charity Tourism Concern runs a campaign to end the 'notoriously exploitative' conditions for locals workers at popular hotels and resorts in some parts of the world. The Sun, Sand, Sea and Sweatshops campaign claims that such hotels are included in the brochures of the UK's four major tour operators. So before you book, ask about your hotel's ethical policy. If this proves difficult to unearth, book your holidays through an ethical operator, such as Responsible Travel, instead (**www.responsibletravel.co.uk**).

STAY OFF THE GREENS Golf courses can use more pesticides than a farmer and have a thirst for water greater than that of a small town. Most golf courses create a huge carbon footprint in an attempt to keep their greens and fairways picture-postcard green – even more so in countries in which water is scarce, such as Spain or Dubai. For the ethical business traveller, a round of golf is generally not a good idea. If you do need your golfing fix, however, look for a course that attempts to minimise its environmental impact. Golf Environment Europe (**www.golfenvironmenteurope.org**), a non-profit organisation working to promote sustainability in golf, may be able to help. And to ease your golfing emissions that teeny bit further, pack some biodegradable golf balls (**www.ecogolfballs.com**) and tees (**www.ecogolf.com**) in your suitcase.

After hours

After work hours the authority of your boss wanes and the opportunity for you to exert your ethical influence over company practices grows. But, whether it is Christmas, an office celebration or a leaving do, the tendency is to equate fun with excess. Over the short Christmas period the UK gets through 750 million glass bottles and jars, 125,000 tonnes of plastic packaging and 83 square km of wrapping paper. Your challenge is to rein in this urge to overindulge without taking the enjoyment out of the proceedings. Fortunately, this isn't hard to do, with green and ethical alternatives to everything from Christmas cards to gin readily available. So, if you have to get wasted, do it without getting wasteful.

Time to party

FIND AN ECO-VENUE **The venue you choose for a party can have a big effect on its environmental impact. Choose a venue with good public transport links, preferably within walking distance of your workplace if it is an office party. Ask the venue if it has an environmental policy, which should cover how it disposes of waste, where its energy comes from and details on the food and drinks it serves.**

USE AN ETHICAL PARTY PLANNER Ethical event-management firms such as London-based Seventeen (**www.seventeenevents.co.uk**) will make sure every element of your party passes the eco test, from the food, the lighting and the sound system to the cherries on top of the fairy cakes.

TOP TIP – RANDY HAYES, FOUNDER OF RAINFOREST ACTION NETWORK
PARTY HARD

To save the planet, you need to work hard and party hard. Work hard to get your office to go green, but when there's an office party, make sure it's green too. When I was President of San Francisco's Commission on the Environment, we wrote the city's Zero Waste Law. We set a target of a 75% reduction of waste to landfill by the year 2010 and of zero waste by 2020. We are already at about 70% reduction now. Of course, we will work hard to get to zero, but imagine the party when we hit that final goal.

THROW A PARTY TO CELEBRATE YOUR ECO ACHIEVEMENTS We talk about setting targets for waste and saving energy as part of your environmental policy in some of the other chapters in this book, and of the need to encourage your staff and colleagues to stick to those targets. Well, if and when you achieve them, why not celebrate by throwing an eco-party? It will be a good excuse to show that being green doesn't have to mean being boring, it can help promote the eco message throughout the company and it can act as an incentive for everyone to continue to improve the company's environmental practices.

AVOID DISPOSABLE PLATES AND CUPS If you think your office will be able to use them again and again, this may be the time to invest in some real plates. If you are ordering lots of wine, you may be able to borrow boxes of glasses from your wine shop – Majestic (**www.majestic.co.uk**) offers this service, for example.

SEEK OUT LOCAL ORGANIC BEER, IF YOU CAN

The average hops farmer uses 15 different pesticides on his crop. However, despite the huge market in organic produce, there are very few organically grown hops in the UK. Most organic beers import hops, so choosing the most eco-friendly beer is usually a toss-up between a locally produced beer, which requires fewer food miles in its production, and an organic beer, which uses fewer pesticides. Duchy Originals Organic Ale is one of the few organic beers made from UK-grown hops, so if you can afford it, this is one of the best beers to lavish on your guests.

TRY ENGLISH WINE As the climate has got warmer in the south of England, more and more vineyards have sprung up. Perversely, this helps our efforts to reduce global warming, as it means we no longer have to import wine, saving on transport emissions. Home-grown organic wine, such as that from Sedlescombe Vineyard in Sussex (**www.englishorganicwine.co.uk**), is now common and is a good choice for the eco-Christmas bash. Even better is biodynamic wine. This takes the concept of organic one step further by using manures and mineral sprays created organically on the same vineyard. It also takes into account the cycles of the moon to create a truly holistic viticultural approach.

BUY FAIR TRADE WINE Wine is not associated with exploited producers in the same way that chocolate and coffee are, but in some parts of the world the treatment of workers on vineyards can be an issue. If you buy wine from South Africa, Chile or Argentina, choose Fairtrade.

FIND A CORKER At the very least, buy wine with real corks. Not a single tree is cut down in their production and, according to

WWF, the cork industry is one of the most environmentally friendly industries possible. This is because it helps maintain the cork forests of Europe, which provide vital habitat for endangered species such as the Iberian lynx and the Barbary ape, as well as providing employment for the people who live there. A cork is also fully biodegradable.

OTHER ALCOHOLIC DRINKS Virtually every drink has an organic variety, from Juniper Green gin (**www.junipergreen.org**) to Highland Harvest organic Scotch whiskey. Organic drinks are generally better for the environment than similar non-organic products, will add a little novelty value to your party and will help promote organic principles.

PARTY FOOD Ever since we were children we have always equated party food with junk food: things like ice cream, crisps and chocolate. Finding eco-friendly party food, therefore, can be a tricky business. If your colleagues can stomach it, put out healthier (yet still tasty) options such as locally grown carrot and celery sticks, roasted chestnuts and strawberries – depending on the season. If you're calling in the caterers for a full-scale feed, then choose an eco-service such as Passion Organic (**www.passionorganic.com**), which specialises in making party food using organic and Fair Trade produce.

A PIECE OF CAKE If your party is to celebrate a birthday, or is for someone leaving the company, the chances are that it will involve a cake at some point. Cakes can be full of chemical colourings and flavourings that leave you feeling a bit sick afterwards. Instead, go for something less toxic, such as a cake from the Organic Chocolate Cake Company (**www.toccc.co.uk**), or the similarly named Organic Cake Company (**www.theorganiccakecompany.co.uk**), which uses local ingredients as much as possible.

PARTY BALLOONS Party balloons are usually made from latex, a natural substance that can be taken from rubber trees without having to cut the trees down. It biodegrades at about the same rate as an oak leaf, so it is a reasonably eco-friendly product. One of the main problems with latex balloons is that when they are released in large numbers as part of a celebration or product promotion, they can end up being swallowed by wildlife and sea animals. If you do want to do a balloon release, the company Ecovy (**www.ecovy.com**) produces balloons made from paper and polyvinyl alcohol, which dissolves when it touches water or moisture. Foil balloons are made from Mylar, a metallicised plastic that doesn't biodegrade, and so these are best avoided.

FLOWERS The boom in the Kenyan flower industry due to airfreighted exports to Europe has been repeatedly picked on as an example of how our extravagance in the West is unnecessarily fuelling climate change. But tackling this issue is not as simple as boycotting flowers produced in Africa. The UK government has defended the Kenyan flower industry, saying that it brings valuable income to the poor east-African country, while research has also found that because the Kenyan flowers are grown outdoors, they actually cause fewer emissions during their lifespan than flowers grown in heated greenhouses in the Netherlands. On the other side of the coin, however, environmentalists are concerned about the levels of pollution in Kenya's lakes and rivers due to the amount of pesticides being used on the flowers. So, what to do? Your best option is to buy local, seasonal flowers – such as daffodils in the spring. Failing that, go for organic flowers if you can find them. Given the choice between Kenyan flowers and out-of-season European varieties, go for the Kenyan ones. Another green option is to hire potted plants and flowers, which can be returned afterwards and reused for other events.

BIOFUEL GENERATOR FOR OUTDOOR EVENTS If you are holding an outdoor event you will probably need to hire a generator to power lights and sound equipment. This is like hiring an engine and leaving it turned on all day, producing a continuous cloud of harmful pollutants, such as CO_2 and carbon monoxide. Depending on your view on biofuels (discussed in chapter 2), you may choose to consider instead a biofuel-run generator, which is carbon neutral – the amount of CO_2 it adds to the atmosphere is the same as the amount it absorbs during its production. Visit **www.midas-uk.co.uk**.

SOLAR-POWERED GENERATOR   Even better than a biofuel generator is a solar-powered generator. The company Wind and Sun Ltd (**www.windandsun.co.uk/exhibitions.htm**) has a mobile generator which it says has been used for stage PA and lighting, radio broadcasts, video projections, computers, recording equipment and… er… sheep shearing. As well as having no fuel costs, a solar-powered generator is silent, so your event doesn't need to be accompanied by the constant hum of an engine. Another company supplying solar generators is Firefly (**www.fireflysolar.co.uk**).

Christmas

DREAMING OF A GREEN CHRISTMAS **Suggest giving the office a green tint this Christmas by avoiding excessive consumerism. Rather than going crazy with gifts, food, decorations and the like, suggest that your company shows its eco credentials by buying less of everything. The money saved can be spent on better-quality food, gifts and decorations that can be used again the following year.**

CHRISTMAS TREES   Cutting down a healthy tree to display in your office for just a few weeks is probably not the most ecologically sound thing you could ever do. But putting up Christmas trees is such an established tradition that it would take only the strongest-minded environmentalist to give them up completely. So what can you do? There is a popular misconception that artificial trees are a greener option, because you can use them again and again. However, these trees usually contain non-biodegradable PVC, and use fossil fuels and release harmful gases into the environment both in production and disposal. At least real trees absorb carbon dioxide during their 'production', rather than give it off. And, of course, they are biodegradable. Although, on the other hand, they are usually grown using harmful pesticides and other chemicals. As you can see, it's a prickly issue. The best option is to find an organic Christmas tree or one with Forest Stewardship Council (FSC) accreditation – there are not many growers, but the Soil Association has a list at **www.soilassociation. org/christmas**. If you can't find an organic tree, at least get one with roots that you can replant after the festive period. The British Christmas Tree Growers Association (**www.christmastree.org.uk**) has a list of suppliers. If you don't have anywhere to replant it, ask your supplier if it will take the tree back and replant it.

RECYCLE YOUR TREE If you do get a cut tree, recycle it. Thousands of tonnes of Christmas trees get dumped in landfill sites each year, even though most councils will collect them and turn them into woodchip to use in public gardens.

GROW YOUR OWN If you can't find an organic Christmas tree with roots, why not grow your own? Ecotopia (**www.ecotopia.co.uk**) sells a Grow Your Own Christmas Tree set, which could make an unusual eco-Christmas present for your clients. However, it takes seven years, on average, for a tree to reach six feet in height, so it may be a few years before it's big enough to act as the official office tree.

NOW FOR SOME DECORATIONS Once you have your tree up, you'll then need some decorations. As with most things connected with Christmas, these are usually environmentally-unsound bits of non-biodegradable plastic produced in polluting factories on the other side of the world, often by poorly paid workers. There are lots of alternatives, however. Ecotopia (**www.ecotopia.co.uk**) sells a range of Christmas tree decorations made from recycled computer circuit boards and recycled CDs and DVDs. WWF (**www.wwf.org.uk/shop**) has a

range of Fairtrade decorations made from long-lasting materials such as porcelain and metal.

MAKE YOUR OWN If you've grown your own tree, why not make your own decorations? Let your imagination run wild. Anything that looks pretty and that you can hang off the branch of a Christmas tree will work, from knitted baubles to old toys.

CHRISTMAS CARDS – WHO NEEDS THEM? Do you work in an office where everyone gives everyone else a Christmas card each year, even if they sit only a few feet away? At the risk of being labelled a killjoy, perhaps you could suggest a pact in which no internal cards are sent. To back up your case you could point out that over 300,000 trees are cut down to make the 1 billion Christmas cards binned in the UK each year. Add to that all the energy used to cut down the trees, turn them into cards and transport them into the shops. Then there is the plastic packaging they often come in. All in all, the waste far outweighs the few seconds of pleasure receiving a card from a colleague sitting at the desk opposite brings.

CORPORATE CARDS The makers of corporate cards will try to tell you that the quality of the card you send to your clients and other business associates says a lot about the quality of your company, and as a result they will try to sell you the biggest, glossiest cards they can. However, with the ever-increasing awareness of environmental issues, the best statement you may be able to make is to not send a card at all. Put a note on your website explaining your decision and the reasons for it.

TOP TIP – RAINFOREST CONCERN
CORPORATE GIFTS THAT DON'T COST THE EARTH
Try to branch out when buying presents for employees and clients with innovative gifts that won't cost the Earth, such as adopting half an acre of rainforest for £25 through the UK charity Rainforest Concern. The donation will be used to purchase and protect some of the most threatened and species-rich rainforests in the world in one of 13 projects run by the charity across Latin America and Asia. Recipients of the gift will get a personalised certificate and will be kept up-to-date about Rainforest Concern projects. For more information, visit **www. rainforestconcern.org** or call 020 7229 2093.

E-CARDS Another green option is to send e-cards. There are literally thousands of e-card websites on the internet, and although they are often tacky, there are good ones to be found if you trawl around, including some that play little funny videos. A couple of my favourites are **www.jimpix. co.uk** and **www.hipstercards.com**. You can also get personalised multi-media cards with your company's name on them, and the website **www. winterwishes.co.uk** will even create corporate e-cards that are interactive games. Add a note explaining the eco-reasons why you are sending an e-card and it could have much more impact than a static, old-fashioned piece of card. And just like real cards, many charities use e-cards to raise funds, so don't worry about not being able to support your favourite cause.

SEND CARDS ON RECYCLED PAPER If you really can't countenance sending anything but cards made of card, at least make sure it is recycled card. Many charities produce cards on recycled paper, so you can make sure the money you spend goes to a good cause.

RECYCLE YOUR CARDS No matter how eco-efficient you are, you are bound to get at least a few Christmas cards in the mail. Don't let the post-Christmas blues distract you from your green ways, however. Remember to recycle your cards after all the festivities are over. The Woodland Trust runs a huge recycling scheme for Christmas cards in which recycling boxes are placed in WH Smith, Tesco and TK Maxx stores across the country. To promote the scheme to your colleagues, the Woodland Trust will send you a campaign poster to put up in your workplace. To get one call 01476 581112 or download it from the Woodland Trust website at **www.woodland-trust.org.uk/cards**.

CORPORATE GIFTS Christmas hampers are a traditional Christmas corporate gift. Show your clients your green side, and at the same time promote organic and Fairtrade produce, by giving ethical hampers at Christmas. Fortunately, organic and Fairtrade goodies are usually of a very high standard in terms of taste and presentation, so your gift is almost certain to  be well received. There are lots of suppliers of ethical hampers, such as The Organic Gift Hamper Company (**www theorganicgift hampercompany.co.uk**) and Simply Fair (**www.simplyfair.co.uk**).

ORGANISE A SECRET SANTA Reduce the need for people in your office to buy all their colleagues small Christmas presents by organising a Secret Santa. Instead of buying lots of presents, everyone in the office anonymously buys a present for one other person, whose name they picked out randomly from a hat. This way, everyone gets a present, and there is a reduction in the amount of wrapping paper required and the number of cheap gifts given that people don't really want. You could also suggest giving the Secret Santa an eco theme to make it even greener. Of course, if you work in an office where nobody gives presents anyway, a Secret Santa will only generate more waste – in which case it would be better not to say anything.

GO CAROL SINGING No batteries are required for this traditional activity. Head out after work a few days before Christmas with a few of your colleagues and sing to the neighbours. If your office is not in a residential area, head out a bit earlier and sing to other offices. It's fun, helps create a sense of community and it helps you get into the spirit of Christmas. You can also raise money for a good cause. The traditional period for singing Christmas carols is from St Thomas's Day (21 December) until the morning of Christmas Day.

 TOP TIP – OXFAM
DON'T BUY UNWANTED CHRISTMAS PRESENTS
At Oxfam Unwrapped, gifts aren't just for Christmas, they're also for life. So, instead of another bottle of champagne for the rich uncle in Ruislip, get a goat for a farmer in Rwanda; instead of a rubber torch for your cousin in Tonbridge, pick condoms to save lives in Tanzania, and rather than splash out on perfume for the maiden aunt in Beaconsfield, provide a much-needed hygiene kit for the emergency workers in Bangladesh. Whether it's animal, vegetable or mineral; practical, medical or educational, **www.oxfamunwrapped.com** offers a different kind of selection of gifts this Christmas, from goats to geological surveys, books to birkads and teachers to toilets.

Eating out

FINE DINING Green dining has suddenly gone upmarket, with fancy new 'eco' restaurants popping up virtually every week. When taking clients out for lunch or dinner, choose an eco-friendly eatery such as Acorn House (www.acornhouserestaurant.com) in London, or Bristol's Bordeaux Quay (www.bordeaux-quay.co.uk). These establishments tick all the right eco boxes, using mainly local, seasonal ingredients, recycling or composting their waste and serving delicious food.

CHOOSE FISH CAREFULLY Hard as it is to believe, the world's vast oceans are rapidly being emptied of fish in order to fill supermarket shelves and restaurant menus. The main problems are over-fishing in certain areas and fishing techniques such as pair trawling and bottom trawling. Bottom trawlers drag enormous nets over the seabed catching things indiscriminately – around half of all bottom-trawler catch is unwanted. Weighted with heavy metal rollers, the nets, some as wide as a football field, smash and crush everything in their path. According to Greenpeace, if the same technique were used on land, it would be like dragging a vast net across the countryside – crushing trees, farms and wildlife in the process – in order to catch a few cows. Bottom trawling has already extinguished as many as 10,000 species. Greenpeace maintains a list of fish species threatened by unsustainable fishing, and it includes many favourites such as Atlantic cod (except line-caught Icelandic), tuna (all species except skipjack), tropical prawns (farmed and wild) and haddock (except line-caught Icelandic). So, before you order fish, ask how and where it was caught.

ASK FOR TAP WATER Various tests conducted by bodies such as the UN Food and Agriculture Organisation have found virtually no difference between bottled water and tap water. Yet, in the UK, we buy three billion litres of bottled water a year, carting it at great environmental expense from the other side of the world in plastic bottles that take hundreds of years to biodegrade. In restaurants, even those people who don't usually buy bottled water feel obliged to order it instead of tap water. Often this is because of the way waiters react when you ask for tap water, with a mixture of pity and reproach. This could have something to do with the fact that bottled water has a higher mark-up price than wine in most restaurants, and so it is in the restaurant's interest to pressure you into buying it. But be brave and ask for tap water. *The Times'* food critic Giles Coren has launched a campaign against restaurants that don't offer tap water 'politely, unsarcastically, and before they offer mineral water', penalising them for it in his reviews. You could make your own protest and eat somewhere else.

UNLESS IT'S BELU The only bottled water Mr Coren will accept is Belu (**www.belu.org**), which comes in a compostable bottle made from corn. The company also donates all of its profits to fund clean water projects both in the UK and around the world. So, if you want to buy a green bottle of water, make sure it's Belu.

CONSIDER THE VEGGIE OPTION The veggie option on a menu is not only for vegetarians. Cutting down on meat as a general rule is good for the environment. According to a study by the UN's Food and Agriculture Organisation, farmed animals produce more greenhouse gas emissions (18%) than the world's entire transport system (13.5%). This may be hard to believe, but a single cow can produce 500 litres of methane a day through flatulence. Methane has 23 times the global warming impact of CO_2, and there are 1.5 billion cows on the planet. Then there are the 1.7 billion flatulent sheep to consider. Add to that all the land cleared for grazing, including huge tracts of the Amazon Rainforest, and all the emissions generated through the manufacture of fertilisers (to grow feed crops), industrial feed production and the transportation of both live animals and their carcasses across the globe, and you have one of the world's most environmentally damaging industries. So, look again at the veggie option to see how palatable it is. And if you're ordering food for an office party or event, consider cutting back on the meat content.

The Boardroom

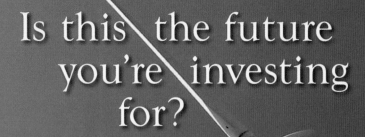

Is this the future you're investing for?

Time to make the
right financial
decisions

www.ethicalinvestors.co.uk

Ethical Investors Group is regulated by the Financial Services Authority

ETHICAL INVEST✺RS

ETHICAL FINANCIAL MANAGEMENT

Business matters

Being seen to be green is good for business. Just witness the number of adverts on television and in newspapers promoting their green insurance, more eco-friendly travel, washing powders that are kind to the planet and even oil refineries that 'grow flowers using waste CO_2'. Yep, green is now good. A recent Mori survey found that 93% of consumers said they thought a company should be responsible for its environmental impact. Not only that, but investors and staff also want to see evidence of your green credentials. So, once you have made the effort to reduce your environmental impact, the next job is to let the world know.

Communications

MAKE SURE YOU HAVE A WEBSITE **If you don't already have a website, get one. And if you do, use it, and keep it up to date. By keeping a good up-to-date website you can significantly reduce the need to use paper and ink for printed publications, reports, marketing materials and any other information you need to communicate. Rather than say, 'I'll pop one in the post', you should be saying, 'Look on our website'.**

KEEP YOUR WEBSITE IN TRIM Of course, a website is not completely emissions-free. For a start, it involves the user spending time on a computer. However, you can reduce the amount of energy (and time) this requires by avoiding flashy graphics and big video files where possible.

THE HOST WITH THE MOST (GREEN SOLUTION) Websites also need to be hosted on an energy-hungry, always-on server somewhere. Reduce your website's emissions by choosing a green hosting service, such as Eco Web Design (**www.ecowebdesign.co.uk**) which uses 100% solar power to run and cool its websites.

DEDICATE SOME SPACE TO BEING GREEN Make sure people are aware of any green initiatives you are carrying out by putting them on your website. If you are doing a fair bit, consider putting up a separate section on your site dedicated to your ethical practices. Even internal schemes, such as using energy-efficient light bulbs in your office, will be of interest to those looking to do business with an ethically minded company.

YOUR INVITATION IS NOT IN THE POST Rather than send out postal invitations to corporate or PR events, printed in ink on paper, placed in an envelope with a costly stamp on the outside, and then driven to the recipient's address, all at great ecological expense, send out e-invites. Put a note at the bottom explaining the eco-reasons why you're not using paper invitations.

RUN ETHICALLY SOUND PR EVENTS To emphasise your green credentials, make an attempt to run any PR events as carbon-neutral as possible – this means picking out a green venue, finding green sound and lighting firms, sourcing green caterers, organic beer, the list goes on. Try to make every single element as sustainable as possible, and make sure your efforts are appreciated by splashing them all over the event marketing material. For help organising a green PR event, contact ethical event company Seventeen (**www.seventeenevents.co.uk**).

Direct your mail

THINK TWICE BEFORE SENDING OUT A MAILING In a poll of the '100 Things That Get Up People's Noses' run by the *Mirror* newspaper, junk mail came 31st, ahead of running out of loo roll and stepping on chewing gum. You may not consider your carefully planned direct marketing campaigns to be junk mail, but many of the people who receive it will. And now, with the increasingly eco-concerns of potential customers, things are getting worse. The Big Green Switch (www.biggreenswitch.co.uk), for example, has started a campaign to reduce the one million tonnes of paper binned as junk mail each year by asking people to sign up to a service that stops them receiving it. So before you send out yet another round of marketing material, consider the environmental implications alongside those financial considerations. The two are increasingly walking hand in hand.

LET THEM SWITCH The Big Green Switch, by asking people to sign up to the Mailing Preference Service to stop them receiving direct mail, is actually doing your business a favour. The service, which is run by the Direct Marketing Association, means that you don't have to waste money, energy and paper sending direct mail to those people most likely to bin it without reading it.

KEEP YOUR MAILING LISTS UP TO DATE Accurately targeting mailing campaigns has, of course, long been a priority for businesses. Now, the increasingly green concerns of businesses and consumers are making it even more important, so make sure you keep those databases up to date. Process returns diligently and check any lists you buy carefully for dud details.

USE RECYCLED PAPER Ninety-five per cent of companies already use paper from recycled or managed resources for their direct mail. If you don't, you should, or you'll be standing out from the crowd for all the wrong reasons.

CHOOSE A VEGETABLE-FRIENDLY PRINTING PROCESS

Non-renewable petroleum, heavy metals and volatile organic compounds – standard mineral-based inks are a concoction of toxic substances. Vegetable-based inks are the greenest option, but only work for sheet-fed litho printing. If you use digital or screen-printing, or need fluorescent inks in litho printing, you will have to use harmful mineral-based inks.

USE BIODEGRADABLE POLYWRAP Plastic has been used for many things in the past because of it durability. So, if you want to send out a free CD or other publicity material with a magazine, for example, the obvious thing to use is polywrap. Unfortunately, the same property that makes it so desirable – its resilience – makes it hard to break down in landfill sites – 90% of all the plastic ever made still exists somewhere today – and makes it dangerous to wildlife. While it is best not to use polywrap at all, if you do, use biodegradable polywrap, which has all the same properties of normal plastic for roughly the same price, except that it can be made to break down in as little as 60 days. Visit **www.degradable.net**.

MAKE IT CLEAR So you have produced a recyclable leaflet, using recycled paper and vegetable-based inks. The next step is to let your customer know, both for promoting your green credentials and to make sure the leaflet gets recycled. WRAP has produced a series of universally recognised 'Recycle Now' logos which you can download for free from

www.recyclenowpartners.org.uk and use in a prominent place on your marketing material.

USE EMAIL Direct email marketing may have an even worse name than direct mail – a recent survey by Yahoo! found that 94% of Britons found spam emails hugely annoying – but at least it is eco-friendly, as there is no paper or delivery required.

Image is everything

GET INVOLVED IN ECO-PROMOTIONS From Fairtrade Week to Bike Week (www.bikeweek.org.uk), there are numerous promotional events you could get involved with to promote your company's green credentials to your clients, customers and staff. During Walk to Work Week, for example, Devon and Cornwall Housing Association offered free bacon butties (organic of course, and there was a vegetarian option for veggies) to all staff who arrived at work on foot. As well as encouraging staff to be green, these initiatives may get picked up in the local, or even national papers, proving invaluable PR for your company.

OFFSET YOUR CARBON On first reading, this looks like a gift to companies wanting to be green without having to do too much to change their business model. Basically you carry on working as before, but every time you do something environmentally damaging, such as taking a flight, you pay a small sum to an offsetting company, they work out how much CO_2 you created and they do something to counteract it, such as planting a tree or installing energy-saving light bulbs in villages in Africa. Sorted. Except…

…DON'T OFFSET YOUR CARBON Environmentalists have come out quite strongly against carbon offsetting and this is beginning to filter into the public's perception, reducing the PR value of offsetting. There are many arguments against it. The first is that it encourages us to carry on polluting the planet when what we should really be doing is causing less waste and pollution. But even if the flight, for example, is unavoidable, there are still reasons not to offset. Some offsetting schemes involve planting trees in developing countries and have been strongly criticised for running plantations where the soil releases more carbon than the trees absorb, and for evicting local villagers from land to plant the trees in the first place.

FINAL WORD ON OFFSETTING   Carbon offsetting is clearly not the pain-free solution to climate change that some companies had been hoping for. However, it can be a useful way to deal with those emissions that can't be avoided. The trick is to be honest about what can and can't be avoided. If you do choose to offset, research your choice of offsetter carefully. And avoid tree-planting schemes – even the director of leading offsetting company Climate Care (**www.climatecare.org**) admitted that such schemes were 'mostly a waste of time and energy'.

BEARING YOUR NAME WELL   If you want to stick your company's name on something, such as a pen or a bookmark, for promotional purposes, make sure it's not produced in a polluting factory somewhere in the developing world where workers rights are abused. It won't exactly be good PR. Better is to source some ethical and environmentally friendly product to bear your name. Eco Marketing (**www.ecopromogifts.co.uk**) offers a range of such products from caps to mugs and even yo-yos.

PUT IT IN A JUTE BAG   If it fits with your business, instead of giving away plastic bags, ask customers to buy a jute bag with your logo on that they can reuse again and again. This will help you build a strong ethical brand and ensure your ethical message is carried around by your customers after they leave your premises. Visit **www.canby.co.uk**.

COMPANY STATIONERY When making all those decisions about cutting down waste and using recycled paper, don't forget all those reams of company stationery and boxes of business cards. A Local Printer (**www.alocalprinter.com**) produces a range of stationery on recycled material – and it will include the recycled logo for free, so that everyone will know how good you are.

BUSINESS CARDS Business cards require paper and ink, so try to be frugal with them. Obviously, this is a matter of common sense; business cards are relatively small and it is not worth losing a valuable lead because you wanted to save a card. Also, use recycled paper and put a recycled paper logo on the back.

Product placement

MAKE YOUR PRODUCTS IN GREEN **Do you produce and sell a product? If you do, look at ways of making it greener. Can you use different materials? Use less materials? Make it run using less energy? Any eco-improvements you make can be trumpeted in the marketing material, helping increase the product's appeal and at the same time improve your company's overall image. The Toyota Prius hybrid fuel car, for example, has been a huge commercial success and has helped put Toyota at the forefront of green driving.**

GO FOR THE GAP Often, by turning your products greener, you may find you have discovered a gap in the market. With consumers and other businesses increasingly looking for the greenest option, by developing a greener product or service you may suddenly find yourself standing out from the crowd. When considering changes you can make, look for the potential gaps in the market. Is there something no one has done yet? Environmental awareness as a mainstream consumer concept is still relatively new and the openings can be plentiful.

CASE STUDY
ADNAMS AND THE WORLD'S LIGHTEST BEER BOTTLE

Suffolk-based brewer Adnams won the 2007 Carbon Trust/*Daily Telegraph* Innovation Awards for embracing energy efficiency across its operations. One of the things Adnams did to save energy was to create the lightest beer bottle on the market. The new bottle reduces Adnams glass usage by 624 tonnes a year and its carbon emissions by 415 tonnes, the equivalent of taking 138 cars off the road. So, as well as gaining lots of positive press attention, Adnams is saving money on glass and energy. Corporate Affairs Manager Emma Hibbert said, 'Reducing our environmental impact is part of the culture at Adnams, so when we had to make some changes at our bottle production plant, we saw it as an opportunity to do something more efficient.'

CORPORATE GIFTS Rather than resort to the dreaded engraved pen or paperweight, give your clients something ethical as a corporate gift. It doesn't have to be a box of energy-saving light bulbs, although that wouldn't be a bad idea. Instead, it could be a bottle of organic

English wine in an ethical jute bottle bag (from **www.canby.co.uk**), or for something a little more unusual, **Tree2mydoor.com** has a range of small trees it says are suitable for business gifts – that may depend on your business, but it's an idea.

GIVE STUFF AWAY ON AN ETHICAL WEBSITE Are you
running a competition to promote a new green product? Ethical Goodies (**www.ethicalgoodies.co.uk**) is a free competitions portal you can use to target ethically conscious consumers.

CASE STUDY
NPOWER'S SOLAR- AND WIND-POWERED ADS

It may be a small gesture in the grand scheme of things, powering outdoor billboard adverts with solar and wind energy, but its marketing effectiveness is brilliant. Right there, next to nPower's latest outside adverts for its wind- and solar-generated electricity product, is proof of its green credentials in the form of highly visible wind turbines and solar panels. As nPower's head of customer marketing said: 'What better way to demonstrate our solar and wind generation products than actively powering poster sites with the energy.' Of course, some might question why a poster needs to be powered at all, but if you think it's a concept worth following up, the billboards were produced by advertising firm Streetbroadcast (**www.streetbroadcast.com**).

CHOOSE AN ETHICAL ADVERTISING AGENCY If you have
made lots of effort to become green, you don't want your endeavours to be trodden on by an unscrupulous advertising agency looking for maximum short-term returns. It may seem like an oxymoron, but there are a handful of advertising firms out there who claim to work in an ethical and sustainable manner. The advertising executives at Tea (**www.theethicalagency.co.uk**) for example, don't even own cars. They compost their office waste and use an ethical printer. For smaller firms,

The Ministry of Truth (**www.mintru.com**) is a Social Enterprise offering high-quality marketing to promote ethical products and services at an affordable price.

DEVISE AN ETHICAL MARKETING STRATEGY When it comes to marketing your company, it is no use just boringly listing all your green credentials. As with any advertising campaign, hitting on the best approach is a tricky business. Try to promote the ethical values that most fit your brand. Also, don't dismiss traditional brand values such as price and quality. It is important to get the right balance, depending on your business and target market.

GO FOR A GREEN AWARD The Green Awards (**www.greenawards.co.uk**) recognise innovative sustainable marketing campaigns, from the clever use of packaging to the best TV ads. Even if your firm's marketing is not up to the standard required to win one of these awards, some of the creative solutions on display could provide the inspiration for a green campaign of your own.

AVOID GREENWASH Make sure your green marketing initiatives don't backfire through short-sightedness. One large energy firm sent out a letter to customers asking them to show their commitment to the environment by signing up for paperless billing. As an incentive, customers who agreed were entered into a prize draw to win cheap flights – hardly the ideal prize for those committed to the environment. The firm was left red-faced when the *Ecologist* magazine published the story under the headline 'Greenwash'. If you are going to promote your firm as ethical, make sure you genuinely are – just paying lip service can go horribly wrong.

Good relations

FORM A PARTNERSHIP WITH A CHARITY **A good way to promote your company's ethical policies is to team up with a charity. There are almost 200,000 charities in the UK, so find one with a strong public image working in a compatible area and work together with it on a relevant project. Charities are keen to form partnerships with ethical companies because it can provide much-needed funds, while companies get to show customers and staff their caring side.**

PRIVATE PUBLIC PARTNERSHIPS As well as teaming up with charities, businesses are increasingly teaming up with local government to tackle climate change. The skills of the commercial sector are being harnessed by the public sector to produce a win-win partnership in which councils get help to implement eco-projects, while businesses get good publicity and recognition within the community. In Newcastle, Australia, for example, the local television station helped the council set up a huge billboard screen in the town centre which monitors and displays the actual energy usage of the town's 15 zones on an hourly basis. This has fostered a competitive atmosphere in the town, with each zone trying new ways to reduce energy use. The TV company reports the results nightly on its news bulletins.

GET LOYAL CUSTOMERS BACK If you are a small local business struggling to compete with the likes of Tesco, you should consider joining a local loyalty card scheme. The Wedge Card (**www.wedgecard.co.uk**), set up by the founder of *The Big Issue*, works just like any big supermarket loyalty card, except that it is for local businesses. Shoppers buy the card and get a small discount when they use it in local shops and on local services. The aim of the card is to revitalise local communities, but there are also lots of environmental benefits from shopping with local businesses. At the moment the Wedge Card only exists in London, but it is looking to expand. Other schemes exist in some local areas around the country.

UP THE JUNCTION Ethical Junction is a network that connects ethical consumers with ethical businesses. On joining, your business is vetted to make sure it is trading ethically. Once accepted you can put the Ethical Junction logo on your marketing material. You also receive free banner ads on the Ethical Junction website (**www.ethical-junction.org**), where your name will sit alongside scores of other ethical companies.

ATTEND GREEN EVENTS Green trade shows such as the Eco Home Show (**www.ecohomeshow.com**) and Ireland's Lifestyle Green Show (**www.lifestylegreen.com**) are a chance to make your presence felt in the ethical marketplace and to connect directly with potential customers, both the public and other businesses. If you are offering an eco-service, or you are an ethically minded business offering a service such as legal aid or accountancy, green events are a useful marketing and networking tool.

SHOW THE PRESS YOUR GREEN SIDE The press is falling over itself these days to find something green to write about. National and regional newspapers, magazines and websites all regularly feature news stories and articles about environmental issues. So, if your company is running an interesting green scheme, or achieving good results with its eco-friendly initiatives, write a press release and spread the word. If your PR agency doesn't seem to understand the value of good green editorial, find an ethical one that does, such as Koan (**www.koanuk.com**).

TOP TIP – GREEN ELEMENT
CONSIDER NOT ADVERTISING YOUR GREENNESS
While promoting all your company's green initiatives up to the hilt may seem like the obvious thing to do, not actively advertising these things has many advantages, too. Promoting your eco-friendly credentials puts you in the spotlight and you will have to be very careful to make sure you live up to your claims. This will include all your dealings with clients – are they green? And what about your suppliers? And their suppliers? Are you ready for your efforts to be scrutinised by environmental groups and the media? British Airways went to great lengths to promote its green values, for example, only for it to get jumped on by environmental groups for starting a new route from London to Cornwall. Lots of negative press followed. Not advertising your eco-initiatives, on the other hand, doesn't mean you can't continue to make the same efforts to reduce your environmental impact and still reap the rewards of improved staff morale and stakeholder confidence. It just means you can do it at your own pace, away from the public spotlight.

One bin day.

Take a look around your office. All those bins, being used for all types of waste without a thought. Take the Envirowise challenge and remove all but one bin from your office for a day. You'll be amazed at how much gets thrown away.

Envirowise offers free, confidential advice to help you start making your business more resource efficient. To find out more, visit **www.envirowise.gov.uk** or call **0800 585794**

enviro**wise**} SUSTAINABLE PRACTICES
SUSTAINABLE PROFITS

Company policy

Environmental and social responsibility is something
employers can no longer afford to take lightly. Not only
are consumers becoming ever more discerning on these
issues, but employees, too, are increasingly considering the
policies of companies before agreeing to join them. Recent
research by BT found that for more than a third of young
professionals, working for a caring and responsible employer
was more important to them than the salary they earned.
In order to successfully fulfil your environmental and social
commitments, and in order to stick to them efficiently and
transparently, you need to create board-level strategies and
get them externally audited. Otherwise, you may find yourself
losing more than just customers.

Management structure

SET UP AN EMS **Any changes you make at any level in your business to limit your environmental impact will need to involve changes to your management practices: adapting your business model to take advantage of new gaps in the market, for example, or ditching your company cars for bikes. Accommodate these changes by setting up an environmental management system (EMS). As well as helping you to reduce your environmental impact, it will help to ensure you comply with relevant legislation, and demonstrate to customers, staff and investors that you are managing your environmental risks and liabilities responsibly.**

ASSESS THE SITUATION The first step in setting up an EMS is to assess your current situation and pinpoint areas where improvement is needed and feasible. This process should also highlight the potential for cost savings and achieving competitive advantage.

THE KEY FEATURES OF A GOOD EMS

To fully contribute to improved environmental performance, a good EMS should:

1. Be implemented at a strategic level and integrated into corporate plans and policies.
2. Identify your impacts on the environment and set clear objectives and targets to improve the management of these aspects as well as your overall environmental performance.
3. Ensure compliance with environmental laws and regulations.
4. Analyse performance and communicate results in a transparent manner.

FROM SMALL ACORNS... A good way of setting up an EMS is to implement the Institute of Environmental Management and Assessment's (IEMA) Acorn scheme (**www.iema.net/acorn**), which provides a

framework for you to follow. The framework has five key phases, which you implement at your own pace. Once you have achieved all five phases, you are ready to apply for the more stringent and complex ISO 14001 standard (see page 181).

BOARD ON BOARD By making a senior manager your company's environmental champion, you will send out a message to your staff that you are taking environmental issues seriously. You will also get more done. Less senior members of staff may be able to encourage colleagues to turn off their computers and recycle waste paper, but to change your business' systems and processes, to set targets and to follow them up, you will have more success if somebody with clout within the organisation takes responsibility.

BE GREEN, BE LAW ABIDING As the UK government and the EU begin to take their role in tackling climate change more seriously, we are likely to see more and more environmental legislation introduced. By being as green as possible you will stay one step ahead of the changes, making compliance easier once they are imposed.

GET THE RIGHT LEGAL ADVICE Environmental legislation, when it does arrive, is often painfully complicated, and so it is wise to seek expert advice. There are many legal firms specialising in environment law, while NetRegs (**www.netregs.gov.uk**) is a government-funded initiative providing free guidance for businesses on how to comply with environmental regulations.

SPREAD THE WORD The final stage in your environmental management process is to ensure the effective communication of your results. Here, the key element is to be transparent and to avoid 'greenwash' (claiming to be greener than you are). Also, it is not just your customers who will want to know what you are doing to be green; your staff, suppliers and other stakeholders will also take a keen interest.

GET ACCREDITED BY EMAS The Eco-Management and Audit Scheme (EMAS) is a Europe-wide scheme to improve companies' environmental performance through management practices in much the same way as the Acorn scheme (page 172) and the ISO 14001 scheme. External certification by any of these schemes demonstrates to shareholders, regulators and the public that your system has been audited, in the same way your financial accounts are audited, by those with appropriate professional skills and knowledge.

JOIN THE INSTITUTE OF ENVIRONMENTAL MANAGEMENT AND ASSESSMENT By becoming a corporate member of the IEMA (**www.iema.net**), you will be demonstrating your commitment to environmental management. In return for your fee you'll receive help in setting up an EMS, free entrance to the institute's events and access to its online library of publications. There is even a free helpline if you need quick advice over the phone.

As a matter of policy

DRAW UP AN ENVIRONMENTAL POLICY **Whatever changes you plan to make in your business – whether it is switching to green electricity or endeavouring to cut down**

on waste – create a coherent environmental policy that can be written up and presented to the public, clients and staff. Making your environmental aims transparent in this way will enhance customer and business relations and will help you achieve your targets. Make your targets realistic and measure your achievements. There is no point setting targets and just forgetting about them. Customers, staff and shareholders will want to see evidence that targets are being met.

KEEP IT SHORT

Follow these few basic rules when drafting your environmental policy:

1. If you want people to read it, which presumably you do, make sure it is not too long – one page should be sufficient.
2. Make sure it is written in plain English.
3. Demonstrate your commitment to your policy by making sure it is signed by the chief executive or another senior manager.
4. Be realistic in the goals you set for your company. Make sure your aims are achievable and relevant to your organisation's activities. There is no point in a printing company, for example, aiming to become paperless, but it would be relevant for a printer to make a commitment to use recycled paper and non-toxic inks.
5. Regularly review your policy to check your company is complying. There is no point saying you are committed to implementing solar power year after year but not doing anything about it. If, on reflection, you have decided against solar power, for example, then amend your policy accordingly.

KEEP STAFF INFORMED Whatever policies you decide to implement, make sure you keep your staff informed by using the company intranet, noticeboards or newsletter. Ask for regular feedback, as they may be bursting with suggestions.

CREATE A TEAM Without your staff on board and involved, your environmental policy will not be worth the recycled paper it's written on. Create a team of people from across the company to include all departments. Let them take charge of projects as much as possible and give them as much time and funds as possible to implement their ideas – remember, most green initiatives will also save you money.

TRAINING Buying this book is a good start, but for maximum success, your team leaders should be fully trained in best environmental practices. There is no point in an employee having the great idea of recycling paper clips if he has no idea about how to go about organising it. Many of the organisations listed in this book run courses in their respective areas of expertise. Envirolink provides free online environmental training via its website **www.epaw.co.uk**.

INCENTIVISE You may be lucky and find you have an entire workforce willing to be eco-friendly purely for altruistic motives. But it is unlikely. The offer of a small incentive, however, may be enough to get the staff working towards a greener future. A monthly prize for the least wasteful department, or a donation to the star employee's favourite charity, for example, may ratchet up the motivation levels.

Social responsibility

BE KIND, CARING AND SHARING **In the hard-nosed world of business, the bottom line is the only thing that counts. Period. You want a life as well? Forget it. You want to care**

about the local community? Don't be soft. But, in reality, businesses have a responsibility to improve their impact on the lives of their staff, their customers, their community and the environment. And in this age of mass communication, those that don't are often brought to account, affecting that all-important bottom line.

COMMUNITY SPIRIT Most big firms will run a programme of community-based initiatives, at least those with a presence in their local community. These could range from sponsoring a local football team to funding tree-planting projects or running a fundraising event for disadvantaged children. Often, schemes are suggested by staff, and businesses put aside a small amount of capital to fund them. Tesco, for example, runs a Computers for Schools initiative, which helps counteract some of the negative publicity it receives by providing local schools with computer equipment.

GIVE YOUR STAFF TIME OFF TO VOLUNTEER According to a survey by Community Service Volunteers (CSV), 92% of people would rather work for a company with an employee volunteering scheme. Offering one, then, would seem a good way to keep your staff happy and to attract high-calibre applicants to your company. There are other benefits, too. Around 59% of employees questioned for the CSV survey said it made them more energised and productive at work. The employers involved were even more positive, with 85% of companies reporting that volunteering helped with productivity, while 42% of firms said it helped reduce the number of staff sick days. Volunteering also gives your staff new skills, which may prove valuable, such as improved communication and diplomacy. Added to all this, a volunteering scheme will contribute to your Corporate Social Responsibility policy and can be good PR. And don't worry, a volunteering scheme doesn't mean losing staff for weeks on end. Just one hour a week can make a big difference. For more information and for help setting up an employee scheme, contact CSV at **www.csv.org.uk**.

TIME FOR A TRANSITION Are you based in a transition town? If you are, get involved. Transition towns are towns preparing for the day when we pass peak oil, when the Earth's finite supplies of oil begin to run out. Some people feel that this day will come within the next few years, and that we need to prepare now by reducing our dependency on oil, our main energy source. The towns each run their own schemes. Totnes, in Devon, for example, has started its own currency, the Totnes pound, to encourage people to spend their money locally. Being part of your local scheme will help you build community relations as well as help reduce your environmental impact. And if your town is not already a transition town, maybe you could start the movement towards it becoming one. For more information visit **www.transitiontowns.org**.

VET YOUR SUPPLIERS If you buy cotton to make T-shirts from a company with a record of mistreating its workers and using dangerous pesticides on its crops, are you, too, guilty of these things? Choose suppliers who have a strong ethical policy and let those with less ethical practices know why you are not doing business with them – as a customer you have the power to affect the policies of other companies. Ask companies for their Corporate Social Responsibility (CSR) or environment policy. If they don't have one, it's not a good sign. Where possible, choose local suppliers to reduce the pollution caused by long-distance deliveries and to help support your local community.

BE KIND TO THE LITTLE MAN Treat your smaller suppliers fairly, they may rely on you to survive. While any business will want to pay the lowest price possible, if you are unscrupulous and squeeze too hard, or fail to pay on time, they may end up going out of business, which will leave you having to look for a new supplier.

TRADE ETHICALLY AND GET CERTIFIED If you source products from the developing world, your CSR policy should include a code of practice covering this. The Ethical Trading Initiative (**www.ethicaltrade.org**) provides a Base Code of minimum standards, which you should adhere to. If you do, you can apply to be certified as an ethical trader.

CASE STUDY
ASDA

When ASDA became the first UK supermarket to ban the use of palm oil in products it sold unless it came from sustainable plantations, the news was picked up in all the national Sunday newspapers. It was a big step, with an estimated one in 10 products sold in the UK containing palm oil (often listed simply as vegetable oil), from chocolate to cosmetics. Friends of the Earth estimates that a region of forest the size of Wales is being cut down in Indonesia alone every year, largely for palm oil. As a result, the survival of many species, including the orang-utan, is under threat. The destruction of the rainforests is also a large contributor to global warming. Although ASDA's ban does not take effect immediately – the supermarket is working with suppliers to help them source sustainable alternatives – by taking the lead on the issue, its green credentials are boosted and it is one step ahead of the game when all the other supermarkets are inevitably forced to follow suit.

DOUBLE CHECK YOUR SUPPLIERS Meeting the requirements of the Ethical Trading Initiative code and becoming certified is not always enough, however. A number of major high-street retailers certified by the Ethical Trading Initiative were recently exposed by a national newspaper for buying products from an Indian firm that employed workers at a rate of just 13p an hour – well below the amount needed to cover their basic needs. The UK companies were as shocked as anyone else and immediately launched internal investigations. The lesson is that as well as getting your code of practice certified by the Ethical Trading Initiative, you should ask tough questions of your suppliers and, if possible, visit their factories yourself to confirm that sufficient standards are being met.

FIND OUT WHO THE GOOD GUYS ARE Subscribe to
Ethical Consumer magazine (**www.ethicalconsumer.org**) or take out a
subscription to one of its online databases – **www.ethiscore.org** for
products or **www.corporatecritic.org** for companies. The magazine
independently researches the social and environmental records of
companies and gives them a rating – it's a bit like *Which?* magazine for
environmentalists. This can help you make an informed decision about
which firms you should be doing business with (or getting supplies from).
Ethical Consumer can also offer tailor-made screening services for more
in-depth information on specific companies, if you want to take it that
step further. Call 0161 227 9099 for more information.

GET LISTED If you think your environmental credentials are quite
strong, make sure you get listed in *Ethical Consumer* magazine and its
online databases. Contact the magazine (**www.ethicalconsumer.org**)
to find out what your environmental policy needs to include in order
to achieve a 'best rating' on its lists. These usually include the creation
of realistic, time-phased targets for getting your company to reduce its
environmental impact.

INVEST IN YOUR PEOPLE Any successful business will know that
a happy, motivated workforce is a productive workforce. But achieving
this may not always be so straightforward. Applying the Investors in
People standard (**www.investorsinpeople.co.uk**) can help. It provides
a framework for businesses to use to improve the skills and motivation
of their staff. It works on the premise that this will lead to increased
productivity, reduced waste and improved customer satisfaction, and that
being a recognised Investor in People will help you attract the best-quality
job applicants.

CONSIDER FLEXIBLE WORKING Keeping with the theme of
a happy workforce, the Equal Opportunities Commission recently ran a
two-year study into flexible and home working and found that it 'could
radically improve' staff and business performance. While the needs of
every business are different, it is worth considering whether flexible or

home working would suit your company. The benefits for businesses include reduced office overheads and improved productivity, recruitment and retention. There are also the environmental benefits derived from having fewer commuters on the roads. BT, one of the chief-proponents of flexible working, claims to have saved employees the equivalent of 1,800 years of commuting time – the equivalent of 47,700 tonnes of CO_2 emissions.

Pats on the back

GET ISO 14001 ACCREDITED **The ISO 14001 is an internationally recognised stamp of approval that lets the world know that under the slick exterior of your company is a well-oiled environmentally conscious management system. The certificate was first thought up at the Rio Earth Summit in 1992 and covers every aspect of how a company is run. To get assessed visit www.british-accreditation.co.uk.**

GET THE GREEN MARK Not quite as stringent as ISO 14001, the Green Mark award (**www.green-mark.co.uk**) is a good place to start in terms of getting an official seal of approval for your environmental efforts. Once you have the Green Mark, which is awarded to small and medium-sized companies committed to on-going environmental improvement, you can put its logo on all your marketing material.

GO FOR AN AWARD If you think your company's eco-credentials are up to it, then put it forward for an eco-award. Today, environmental credentials are highly valued by the public and winning an award is brilliant PR. Your own employees will hopefully also feel proud of the achievement and will feel driven to maintain and even improve good environmental work practices. Most industries and sectors have their own awards, with many including eco-categories, but for maximum glory you could go for either the Carbon Trust/*Daily Telegraph* Innovation Awards (**www.carbontrust.co.uk/innovation_awards**) or the Ecover/*Observer* Ethical Awards (**observer.guardian.co.uk/ethicalawards**). The fact that both are sponsored by national newspapers means good press coverage is guaranteed.

BECOME A MAY DAY COMPANY On 1 May 2007 over 1,000 business leaders gathered together to pledge action on climate change, forming a national movement known as the May Day Companies. Any company can join the movement by making one or more of a number of environmental pledges, from measuring your emissions to providing information to your customers about your carbon footprint. May Day Companies pledge to report back on their progress at subsequent May Day meetings in 2008 and beyond. Visit **www.bitc.org.uk/what_we_do/may_day**.

Conference call

Despite the advance of communications technology in the form of mobile phones, the internet, video conferencing facilities and so on, our reliance on transport to physically move people and things around shows no sign of abating. In fact, transport accounts for roughly a quarter of emissions in the UK and is the fastest-growing source of climate change gases. As a business trying to become green, your task is simple: to reduce your emissions. Look at how your staff travel to work and to meetings. How are deliveries made? In most cases there are greener options. No one solution will fit every situation – bikes are no good for delivering heavy goods, for example – and so a range of transport solutions will need to be used. For some ways to start, turn the page.

Freight

GET OFF THE ROAD **With road freight accounting for 8% of the UK's CO_2 emissions, any responsible business should consider finding a more environmentally friendly alternative. HGV lorries also contribute to congestion, damage the roads, leading to costly repairs and yet more congestion, and they are dangerous. Government research found that when large lorries are involved in accidents the level of injury tends to be higher – HGVs are twice as likely to be involved in fatal accidents as cars.**

FREIGHT TRAIN An average freight train can remove 50 to 60 HGVs from the roads, producing between five and 10 times fewer emissions. It's a statistic that is catching the eye of more and more businesses, with ASDA, Argos and Superdrug all recently increasing the amount of goods they transport by train. The government is so convinced of the benefits of moving freight by rail that it has set a target of an 80% increase in the use of rail freight, from 2000 levels, by 2010. For more details on rail freight, visit **www.freightonrail.org.uk**.

BACK TO THE FUTURE One hundred years ago, many businesses transported heavy goods along Britain's extensive network of canals. Today, after years of innovation, traffic jams and pollution, canals are coming back into fashion. The latest firm to jump on board is supermarket giant Sainsbury's. The company ran a one-month trial in which goods were delivered to one of its London stores by barge. Supply chain director Roger Burnley said the trial proved there were alternatives through which companies can become more efficient, environmentally sustainable and to cause less congestion on busy roads. 'It's interesting that one of the ways we could do this is by revisiting how we operated when we set up shop almost 140 years ago,' he said. However, despite the trial's success, Sainsbury's has no immediate plans to replace its lorries with boats, due to the huge infrastructure changes it would involve. If you have a smaller company, however, perhaps it is something you could consider. For information on transporting your freight by canal, call British Waterways (**www.britishwaterways.co.uk**) on 01923 201120.

TURN WHITE VAN MAN GREEN The Modec van is an electric van about the size of a typical 'white van'. It produces no emissions and can carry two tonnes up to 100 miles at 50mph on a single charge. Run it on green electricity and it is virtually zero-carbon – apart from the energy used to manufacture and maintain it. Although it costs as much as an equivalent diesel vehicle to run – as you have to lease the battery – it is exempt from road tax and London's congestion charge, it is in a low insurance band and there is no requirement for an operator's licence. It is also virtually silent, which is useful if you need to make early-morning deliveries in built-up areas. Visit **www.modec.co.uk**.

GREEN LORRIES A white van not big enough for your purposes? Smith Electric Vehicles (**www.smithelectricvehicles.com**) produces a range of electric lorries, the biggest of which, the Smith Newton, can carry up to 7.5 tonnes up to 130 miles at 50mph on a single charge. Marks & Spencer is leading the converts, with Royal Mail also trialling the Smith Newton in London. Even former Prime Minister Tony Blair was impressed. 'In years to come, this operation is absolutely where the future will be,' he said.

TOP TIP – INTERNATIONAL FUND FOR ANIMAL WELFARE (IFAW)

USE A CARBON-NEUTRAL COURIER

When choosing to use a courier, research companies that are carbon neutral and based close to your office. Certain companies offset emissions by investing in projects that help the environment. In cities, instead of using a motorbike or van courier, use a cyclist where possible. You may find they will be more cost effective – and they can even be quicker in heavy traffic.

BRING IT IN BY BOAT According to the Chamber of Shipping, shipping is 'by a long way the most energy-efficient – and the least environmentally damaging – form of transport'. Which is good news, as over 90% of the world's trade is carried by ships. According to the influential 2007 Stern Report, shipping and rail combined produce only 1.75% of greenhouse gas emissions, compared with 10.5% for road transport. So, if you need to bring anything in from across the seas, check with your suppliers that it is coming by boat, and not being flown or driven across Europe.

ALTERNATIVE FUEL If you do have to use non-electric lorries to transport goods, you can still make an eco choice through the fuel you use. A recent survey by the Freight Transport Association found that 25% of lorry operators have already switched from petrol and diesel to biodiesel. While this fuel can be controversial, depending on where the plants used to make it are grown (see The Commute chapter), it is virtually carbon neutral. Another feasible alternative fuel is liquid petroleum gas (LPG), which, while it is still a fossil fuel, has lower carbon dioxide emissions than petrol (it produces more carbon dioxide than diesel, but less nitrous oxide and particulates). It is also currently cheaper because it has a lower fuel duty. You can usually convert your lorry so that it will run off either LPG or diesel at the flick of a switch.

TEACH YOUR DRIVERS TO DRIVE GREEN Simple things like checking your tyres regularly and changing gears at the optimum moment can save fuel and so reduce your environmental impact. Send your delivery drivers, regardless of the size of their vehicle, on a green driving course, such as the Fuel Efficiency Driving course run by the Transport Training Academy (**www.transporttrainingacademy.co.uk/ Fuel-Efficient-Driving.html**).

Company cars

BENEFIT OF THE PLANET A company car may be vital for some people, but for those who don't really need it for work purposes, offer another staff benefit instead, such as private health insurance or gym membership.

FLEETS OF GREEN While owning a fleet of company cars is unlikely to win you many environmental awards, the type of cars you buy can significantly affect your green credentials. The government recently launched a website (**www.dft.gov.uk/ActOnCO2**) to inform buyers of the greenest models in each class of vehicle. So, for example, the Volkswagen Polo Blue Motion is currently the least-polluting car in the super-mini class, producing just 99g of CO_2 per km. As a general rule, cars with smaller engines produce less pollution and are cheaper to run. However,

even if an executive car is the only thing for you, the government website means you can still choose the greenest model available. In the executive class, for example, the BMW 5 Series E60/E61 tops the list, producing 136g of CO_2 per km.

LITTLE WONDER It may not be to everyone's taste, and it has some distinct disadvantages (like a top speed of only 45mph), but the G-Wiz electric car is just about the greenest thing on four wheels. Not only that, it's incredibly cheap to run (from as little as 1.3p per mile), and it is exempt from road tax, the London congestion charge and most parking charges in central London. Run it on electricity generated by renewable energy and it is virtually zero-carbon.

 TOP TIP – CARPLUS
CAR CLUB TOGETHER

Car clubs can easily replace an existing company fleet. They offer pay-as-you-go access to a vehicle whenever you need it. Cars are booked via the telephone or the internet and are administered by an operator. Companies can block-book vehicles during office hours, leaving the cars free for local residents at evenings and weekends. Joining a car club will not only save your company money and time administering bookings and cleaning the cars, it will also improve your green credentials as staff can instead commute by public transport, walking and cycling and still have use of a car for work purposes. It also means there are less cars on the road, and they are used more efficiently.

SCRAP ANY FREE FUEL POLICIES Providing free fuel for the private use of staff is expensive and damaging to the planet. Senior management often benefit most from free fuel, so you may encounter some resistance to change. If this is insurmountable, perhaps you could phase the policy in by applying it just to new employees. Or change any petrol allowance to a mileage allowance to avoid giving an advantage to those driving the most inefficient vehicles.

GO LOCAL Green up your act by going local. Why do business with an organisation based miles, or even continents, away when you could be doing business on your own doorstep? Depending on your size, this could mean a commitment to sourcing goods and services from the same town, county or even country in which you are located. Local suppliers will be hungry for your business. Invite them to pitch and you could be surprised by the benefits, not just in terms of sustainability, but also in terms of quality, innovation and nimbleness of response. Going local is a simple but powerful way of demonstrating your commitment to the environment.

Corporate travel

ASSESS YOUR SITE'S ACCESS **Drawing up a packet of green travel measures tailored to your particular site can, according to the Campaign for Better Transport (formerly Transport 2000), reduce commuter car transport by up to 30%. Your travel plan should cover how everyone, from your staff and visitors to contractors and fleet vehicles, travels to and from your workplace. Pharmaceutical firm AstraZenica, for example, first introduced a travel plan at its Alderley Park site back in 1998. It began by holding staff focus groups, and as a result implemented a plan to bring services such as dry-cleaners and banking on-site, set up a car-sharing scheme, and subsidise bus routes. For more advice on setting up a travel plan, go to www.dft.gov.uk/pgr/ sustainable/travelplans/work/essentialguide.pdf.**

EMPLOY A TRAVEL PLANNER If you are a large company, or you do a lot of travelling, it may be worth employing a travel planner to draw up and implement your company's travel plan. By leaving it to someone who is already working full-time on something else, you may miss out on the full spectrum of financial and environmental benefits.

STAY IN THE OFFICE A good business will already assess whether each journey it makes is strictly necessary, but concerns are usually only centred on the financial implications of travel. Factor in environmental concerns as well, as an added incentive to come up with alternative ways of conducting business.

DON'T FLY TOO HIGH The Institute of Travel Management has got together with a number of well-regarded institutions, including Cambridge University and the Airline Environmental Federation, to produce a toolkit for sustainable business travel. The government-funded project, called Icarus, is available to businesses to download for free from **www.itm.org.uk/icarus** and is packed full of useful guidance on creating an environmental travel plan.

 **TOP TIP – ASSOCIATION FOR COMMUTER TRANSPORT**

ACTION PLAN

The commute to work is the most frequently omitted consideration in an organisation's quest to be green. It is usually sidestepped by organisations, who claim that 'how employees get to work is not our responsibility'. But transport accounts for over 20% of emissions and, if we continue to ignore the impact, by 2050 it will account for 100% of targeted greenhouse emissions in the EU. The good news is that catering for sustainable transport will also save you money. Parking spaces in the UK are valued at between £700 and £3,000 per space per annum. Why provide this free bonus to staff who drive without considering other options? Instead, implement a travel plan. This should begin with a survey of your staff and visitors to see where they commute from, and then provide incentives for them to use other modes of transport. Travel plan measures can include things like cycle facilities or discounted rail or bus tickets. It is imperative to not just provide alternatives, but to encourage staff to use them. Many companies have succeeded in encouraging a high take up through prize draws, parking charges, or simply providing clear information on how to do it.

SHUTTLE BUS If your office is located away from any regular bus routes, you could consider laying on a shuttle bus for staff and visitors. When the National Trust moved its offices from Cirencester and Westbury to Swindon, it ran a daily bus between the towns for people who didn't want to relocate. Not only will a company bus cut down on the amount of cars on the road and the number of parking spaces you require, but, providing you lay on a good service, it will guarantee that your staff arrive to work on time.

CONFERENCE WITH GOOD LINKS If you are holding a conference, consider how people will get there. Pick a venue in a central location and with good public transport links. If the conference has an entrance fee, you could offer a discount to people who arrive by bike or public transport – the boost to your green credentials will go some way to counteracting any loss in income.

DON'T TRAVEL, VIDEOCONFERENCE You may consider a deal not a deal until hands have been firmly shaken, but with the advance of ever-improving videoconferencing facilities, that attitude is increasingly becoming old-fashioned. A recent study found that a third of UK employees thought face-to-face meetings were not only unnecessary, but also counter-productive. Why battle through congestion

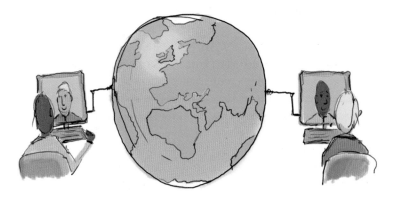

to an airport, undergo vigorous and time-consuming security triple checks, sit on a carbon-spewing plane and jump in a taxi in a foreign country, when you could instead have a five-minute videoconference call, saving huge amounts of time, money and environmental damage? For a list of videoconference facilities across the UK visit **www.itm.org.uk/icarus/icarus_tool7.asp**.

JUST DON'T ALL TALK AT ONCE If you don't want to invest in expensive videoconferencing equipment, some face-to-face meetings could be replaced with teleconferencing. This requires no additional equipment, simply a telephone for each person – most phone companies will have the service available to its customers. Simply book a session and give everybody who needs to take part the necessary access numbers they need to dial in.

GET PEOPLE NETWORKING BEFORE THEY EVEN ARRIVE
One of the main reasons people go to conferences is to network. Why not aid this process and at the same time save on transport emissions by helping people team up to travel together to your event, such as by sharing a hire car. The website **www.spaceshare.com** will set up a special online database for your event through which attendees can link up. As well as transport, it helps people cut down on resources by sharing hotel rooms – although that may be going a bit far for most people.

MAKE YOUR CONFERENCE GREEN When putting on a conference, make sure you speak to the venue about your environmental concerns. There is no use promoting your green credentials only for clients to turn up at your conference and find empty rooms with lights and air conditioning left on, food offered in excessive packaging or a lack of recycling facilities. BlueGreen Meetings (**www.bluegreenmeetings.org**) is a North American charity offering advice on running an environmentally friendly conference and has lots of tips on getting it right.

ECO CONFERENCE WITH A DIFFERENCE If you want to run an environmentally friendly conference that stands out you could hold it at

Green & Away (**www.greenandaway.org**), Europe's only tented conference centre, in Worcestershire. All the buildings (sorry, tents) are eco-friendly, low-impact structures that get put away at the end of the summer season. The kitchen tent is powered by solar energy and uses produce from the venue's own organic vegetable garden, and there is even a bar selling organic beer and wine.

 CASE STUDY
AMICUS

Manufacturing union Amicus has begun introducing videoconferencing in a bid to cut down its annual £1.5 million bill for travel expenses and to improve its environmental impact. Amicus has 38 sites across the country, with people regularly travelling to London for two or three-hour meetings. The union recently held an event where the general secretary addressed 200 people in 20 offices via videoconference. In the past, all those people would have had to travel to London from as far away as Aberdeen, causing a huge drain on resources.

Staff travel

SUBSIDISE PUBLIC TRANSPORT **It may give your finance director heart palpitations, but subsidising your employees' public transport costs is a good way to encourage them to travel in a more environmentally friendly way. It will also promote your green credentials and can help with recruitment and retention of staff. On top of that, it can save you the costs of keeping and maintaining parking spaces.**

NEGOTIATE A DISCOUNT If you can convince your local transport operator that your staff are keen to use public transport, you may be able to negotiate a discount, which you can then pass on to staff as a benefit.

Depending on how large a company you are, you may even be able to convince them to change their bus routes and timetables to fit with when your staff leave and arrive at work.

SEASON TICKET LOANS If subsidising your staff's public transport usage is a step too far, you could instead provide a season ticket loan. This will ease the pressure on staff having to pay out a big lump sum in advance. Instead, you loan them the money and they pay it back to you in instalments – interest free, of course.

CATER FOR CYCLISTS Not only is cycling extremely environmentally friendly, but, according to the British Medical Association, cyclists have lower levels of stress and have a fitness level equivalent to someone 10 years younger. They also take fewer days off sick. If this sounds like the kind of healthy workforce you want to encourage, then cater for people cycling to work. Provide ample secure space, preferably covered, for people to park their bikes.

GET TAX BREAKS The government has begun offering tax breaks and incentives for employers that promote the joys of cycling to staff. These range from incentives on setting up cycle parking facilities to tax breaks on safety equipment, such as lights and helmets. Visit CTC, the UK's national cyclists' organisation, at **www.ctc.org.uk** for more information.

SHOWER THEM IN GIFTS If you're really serious about encouraging cycling to work, you should think about providing showers and clothes lockers. The thought of turning up to work all hot and sweaty, or with work clothes wet from the rain, is one of the main factors putting people off cycling. If you have the space, showers and lockers will solve this problem.

BIKE MILEAGE Setting up a cycling mileage allowance scheme, along the lines of a car mileage allowance, may seem like giving away money, but with cycle miles cheaper than car miles (20p per mile, compared with 40p per mile), for each worker that switches, you'll actually be saving money.

CASE STUDY

GLAXOSMITHKLINE BIKE MILES SCHEME

Pharmaceutical giant GlaxoSmithKline runs a scheme rewarding staff who arrive at work on a bike with a £1 voucher, redeemable at Evans Cycles or with the company's cycle mechanic, Dr Bike, who attends the site every two weeks. GSK pays Dr Bike for his time and so staff just pay for any parts needed. As a result of the scheme, the number of employees registered as cycling to work at GSK House, their headquarters in Brentford, has risen to more than 370, which is more than 10% of staff. Joss Mathieson, a director in the company's media team, says that the success of the cycle to work scheme has undoubtedly eased pressure on parking spaces at the site. 'We have a restricted number of spaces here, significantly fewer than the number of employees working here,' he explains. 'Consequently, the site operates a rotation policy whereby one week in every five you cannot park on site. The success of the bike scheme in encouraging people to cycle to work has eased the pressure on spaces sufficiently that we now operate a "parking lottery", where a proportion of the people on their "no parking week" will win a space back.'

LOBBY FOR BETTER LANES AND LIGHTING One thing that puts many people off cycling is the fact that it is quite dangerous – almost 2,500 cyclists are killed or seriously injured in the UK each year. You can do your bit as a company to alleviate this worry by adding your voice to those of cycle campaigners in the area, such as the London Cycling Campaign (**www.lcc.org.uk**), or approaching your local council about improving things like cycle lanes and lighting near your workplace.

POOL OF BIKES Consider setting up a bike pool for staff who don't own bikes. A bike pool provides staff with the free use of well-maintained bikes. They can be used for any kind of journey, but usually they are reserved for work-related trips, such as local meetings, travel between sites and visiting clients.

POOL CARS TOO If you can pool bikes, then why not pool cars too? By having a small number of cars on hand for those employees who need to drive either for meetings or for other business purposes, you can reduce the need for staff to bring their cars to work. Instead, you can encourage them to use a greener form of transport, such as cycling or taking the bus. A car pool could also reduce the need for take-home company cars and parking spaces.

BECOME A CYCLE-FRIENDLY EMPLOYER If all this talk of cycling has you bamboozled, Life Cycle UK has set up a website for those managers with little interest or understanding of cycling, explaining the benefits of becoming a cycle-friendly employer. The web address is, helpfully, **www.cyclefriendlyemployers.org.uk**.

SIGN UP FOR ECO BREAKDOWN COVER The Environmental Transport Association actively encourages people to use their cars less. It may not seem like sound business sense for a breakdown service reliant on car users for its income, but the ETA has a long history of campaigning for a more sustainable transport system. In 1992 it started Green Transport Week and it runs National Car Free Day every year. As well as offsetting all of its business emissions, the company is run according to strict environmental and ethical policies. So, when you come to sign your company fleet up for breakdown cover, look beyond the big two for a greener alternative. Visit **www.eta.co.uk**.

 TOP TIP – RESPONSIBLETRAVEL.COM
RESPONSIBLE BUSINESS TRAVEL
When planning your holiday or business trip, make sure you plan your route so as to minimise your carbon emissions as much as possible. Take fewer and longer holidays, take the train to European destinations and consider UK-based eco-holidays. Responsibletravel.com has a range of 'I don't want to fly' holidays. If you do fly, avoid short flights and stopovers, as the worst carbon emissions are emitted during take off and landing. However, for those flights that you cannot avoid, be sure to offset the carbon emissions of your flight. That way the money is invested in effective carbon-reducing initiatives around the world. At your destination, travel by train and public transport wherever possible and cut down on internal flights. You'll often experience more of a country and culture and have a more memorable journey by taking local buses or trains instead. Alternatively, consider hiring a bike, a canoe or even walking! Go to **www.responsibletravel.com** or call 01273 600030.

GET YOUR STAFF WALKING Regular walking will improve the health of your staff and help them to feel part of the local community. As well as reducing the number of days they take off sick, their presence in the local area will help your company forge good local relationships. The organisation Urban Walks (**www.urbanwalks.co.uk**) will help you organise walking activities for your staff by providing advice and leaflets about walking. And don't worry about productivity levels if all your staff are out taking a stroll, as all the activities can take place during lunchbreaks. Besides, regular exercise will actually increase concentration levels and reduce stress when your staff are in the office.

Environmental Practice at Work Co Ltd helps you organise
environmental improvements in your workplace. We have a range of
programmes for all levels within your organisation dealing with all aspects
of sustainability.
Look at these free materials:

Environmental Practitioner Toolkit
www.epaw.co.uk/EPT
Sustainable Food Procurement Guide
www.sustainablefood.com/guide
Carbon Counter Toolkit
www.carboncounter.info/toolkit.html
Environmental Awareness Scheme for Employees for ISO 14001
www.epaw.co.uk/ease.html (sample)
Health and Safety Practices
www.healthandsafetypractices.co.uk
Corporate Social Responsibility Planning and Reporting Guide
www.epaw.co.uk/csr

All materials are developed using nationally and internationally recognised
skills, systems and standards. We customise these for your particular needs,
and can add On-line databases and make individual Scorm compliant
learning modules.

For details of free sites and customised learning materials contact
info@epaw.co.uk Tel: +44(0)1254 381289

*Environmental Practice at Work Publishing Company Limited. Registered Office 10 Mayville Road, Pendle,
Lancashire, UK tel: +44 (0)1254 381289
Company registered in England in Wales: Registered Company Number 3718623
VAT Registration Number: 759 3051 17 Registered under the Data Protection Act: Registration Number
Z5338711*

Move with the times

Buildings not only account for roughly half of all the UK's CO_2 emissions, they also make people sick. Sick Building Syndrome has been officially recognised by the World Health Organisation since 1982, and can cause sore throats, persistent coughs, blocked noses, stiff shoulders, back ache, tiredness, headaches and digestion disorders. Hardly the recipe for a happy and productive workforce. Interestingly, most of the factors contributing to Sick Building Syndrome also contribute to environmental damage, such as air conditioning, a lack of natural lighting, the use of solvent-based paints, and chemical pollutants from things like printers and furniture. The way you design, refurbish and kit out your office will affect the cost of running the building, its impact on the environment and the health of your staff.

New building design

NEW VS OLD **If you're thinking of moving into a new premises, is it more environmentally sound to move into an existing building, or construct a new one from scratch? This is an interesting question that has no definitive answer as yet – although the Empty Homes Agency (www.emptyhomes.com) is running a study that aims to provide one. By recycling an existing building you are avoiding all the energy and waste associated with construction. However, it is much easier to create an energy-efficient new building than make an old building efficient. New buildings are now being designed that are so well insulated, and make such good use of light, alternative energy sources and environmentally-sound materials, that they are carbon-neutral – meaning they generate as much energy as they use.**

LET IN THE SUNLIGHT It is common sense that a dark office with small windows will need to use more electricity for lighting than a bright one. A building can also obtain over half of its heating needs through clever use of 'passive solar' design methods. That doesn't mean making the office entirely out of glass, as this will cause heat-loss problems in winter and may require huge amounts of air conditioning in the summer. Instead, simple techniques, such as using glass flooring to let light permeate multiple levels and using open stairwells, maximise the use of available light. Light-coloured walls will also make a room brighter.

USE LIGHT TUBES Pipe in daylight to those dark areas where windows aren't viable using light tubes. These highly reflective tubes 'collect' light, usually through a hole in the roof, and transport it into your building where a diffuser spreads it around a room. In optimum circumstances, light tubes can provide as much light as a 500-watt bulb, but they will also work even if you have to bend them around corners. Visit **www.solalighting.co.uk**.

CASE STUDY
NATIONAL TRUST OFFICE

The National Trust's new headquarters in Swindon is a beacon of environmentally friendly architecture. The organisation previously had offices in four different sites, with many staff needing to travel regularly between them for meetings, so having one central office has reduced costs and pollution. The building itself – called Heelis – makes maximum use of daylight and uses natural ventilation, reducing lighting and air-conditioning needs. The office is expected to generate just 15kg of carbon dioxide per square metre per year compared to 169kg for a typical air-conditioned office. Around 40% of the building's electricity needs are met by 1,554 solar panels on the south-facing pitched roof, and in the building's reception a display monitor shows staff and visitors the amount of energy generated by the panels and the CO_2 emissions saved. Even the carpet has been specially developed for the building using wool from sheep grazed on National Trust farmland.

BREEAM YOUR PLANS BREEAM is an internationally recognised environmental assessment method for buildings. The scheme gives an official seal of approval to environmentally sound developments, but also helps designers to reduce the environmental impact of their projects. While it can be used to assess existing buildings, it is best to get an assessment during the design stage in order to make sure any environmental improvements identified can be incorporated as it is being built. Visit **www.breeam.org**.

FIND OUT WHICH MATERIALS WOULD BE MOST EFFECTIVE FOR YOUR BUILDING Incorporating sustainability

into a building's design, and matching it against the costs and cost savings over the life of the building, is a complex process. Envest 2 (**envestv2. bre.co.uk**) software offers some help. It lets designers input their plans and shows what the effect on the building's environmental impact and whole-life costs would be as a result of using different materials. It can also predict the environmental and cost implications of using various methods of heating, cooling and operating a building.

INCORPORATE TIMBER INTO YOUR DESIGN Around 60% of the construction industry's energy consumption is used in producing materials. Most of the energy used to produce timber comes from a renewable source, the sun, and so using wood helps reduce a building's carbon footprint. Wood also looks nice in a building, but make sure it comes from sustainably managed forests by looking for the FSC-approved mark issued by the Forest Stewardship Council.

USE LOCAL MATERIALS The Snowdonia National Park Authority provoked a local outcry when it imported stone from Portugal for the roof of the new visitor centre on the top of Snowdon. Avoid the same mistake. Help local businesses and cut down on transport emissions by using a local stone or timber rather than importing materials from abroad.

TOP TIP – EDWARD BULMER
OFFICE GIVING YOU A HEADACHE?
Your office is likely to be re-painted with synthetic paints every couple of years. For about five years after application these paints will 'outgas' leading to 'passive paint inhalation'. This is a contributor to 'sick building syndrome' associated with headaches and eye, nose and throat irritation. Save yourself a headache and choose a natural solution, which is hard-wearing and durable. Edward Bulmer's Pots of Paint colour range is totally natural with no synthetic solvents, no Volatile Organic Compounds, no harmful emissions, they involve practically no waste and use only raw materials from sustainable sources. Visit **www. edwardbulmer.co.uk** or telephone 01544 388 535.

Harnessing energy

SWITCH TO GREEN ELECTRICITY **Whatever business you are in, you can switch your electricity supply from**

carbon fuels to clean energy, such as wind or solar power. To do this you don't have to climb up on your roof and install some expensive device. Simply call a green energy provider, such as Ecotricity (www.ecotricity.co.uk), and within a few minutes all those resource-hungry computers will be set to run on clean, renewable wind, solar or hydro power. For the full range of suppliers in your area, both green and non-green, visit www.uswitch.com.

USE SOLAR POWER In a single hour the sun transmits more energy to the Earth's surface than humankind uses in a year, but we don't get close to making the most of this free and plentiful resource. As well as using its energy directly for light and heat through your windows, you can harness the sun to generate clean electricity by installing photovoltaic (PV) solar panels on your roof. The high visibility of PV panels will also act as a public display of your company's commitment to the environment.

FEEL THE HEAT If the high cost of installing photovoltaic panels to produce electricity puts you off consider, instead, installing a solar hot water system, which is cheaper and could reduce your energy bills by up to 5%. The Low Impact Living Initiative runs a weekend course on how to build a solar water heater, at the end of which you take home a custom-made system to install. Visit **www.lowimpact.org**.

WIND POWER A wind turbine can generate clean renewable electricity and stand tall and visible as a symbol of your commitment to reducing the environmental impact of your business. However, you need to be in a reasonably windy location in order for a turbine to work effectively. If your office is surrounded by trees, or is sheltered by larger buildings or a hill, then a wind turbine is not for you. For more information visit **www.lowcarbonbuildings.org. uk/micro/wind**.

HEAT FROM THE EARTH Ground source heat pumps take heat from under the ground and use it to heat your office. Regardless of the temperature above ground, below the surface the temperature is maintained at between 10°C and 14°C. The system requires an electrically driven pump to move the heat, so unless you use green electricity, it will still cause some CO_2 emissions. However, your emissions will be much less than if you heat your office using traditional methods. For more information, visit the website of the Ground Source Heat Pump Association at **www.nef.org.uk/gshp**.

TAKE A DIP IN THE RIVER If you happen to have a fast-moving stream or river running by your office, it may be possible to use it to generate electricity. Unlike solar or wind power, hydropower can be generated constantly – unless there is a drought. Even small hydro schemes have the capacity to generate substantial amounts of electricity, and you may be able to make money by selling some back to your electricity company. Visit **www.hydrogeneration.co.uk**.

INSTALL A BIOMASS BOILER Another renewable energy source that can be used to heat your office is biomass. Sometimes called biofuel or bioenergy, biomass is organic plant matter, such as wood or straw. Unlike burning fossil fuels, burning biomass is carbon neutral as the CO_2 produced is equal to the CO_2 absorbed from the atmosphere during the plant's life. As you have to buy the fuel, the cost of a biomass boiler will depend on your local fuel source. To make it even more environmentally sound, biomass can be generated from organic waste which would otherwise be sent to landfill. For more information, visit **www.biomassenergycentre.org.uk**.

CASH INJECTION The government's Low Carbon Buildings Programme offers businesses grants of up to £1 million to install renewable energy systems, such as solar panels, wind turbines or ground source heat pumps. Too good to be true? Well, maybe. The government has been heavily criticised for allocating too little money to the scheme – it is spending over 30 times as much on widening a stretch of the M6 motorway. However, if you fancy your chances of securing a grant before the scheme closes in April 2009, the application forms and information can be found at **www.lowcarbonbuildings.org.uk**.

INTEREST-FREE LOAN If a grant proves too difficult to lay your hands on, you may have better luck with an interest-free loan of up to £100,000 from the Carbon Trust. The scheme has a wide remit and covers any carbon-cutting improvements, which could include things like fitting energy-efficient boilers, as well as installing renewable energy systems. The loans are for small and medium-sized enterprises only (companies with less than 250 employees) and should be repaid within five years with money saved on your energy bill – you'll need to show you can do this to secure the loan. For more information, visit **www.carbontrust.co.uk/energy/takingaction/loans_renewables.htm**.

Relocation, relocation, relocation

DON'T PAVE OVER THE COUNTRYSIDE **An office with countryside views may feel very eco-friendly, but you should avoid building on green open spaces. As well as contributing to urban sprawl by concreting over nature, it is more likely your employees will have to travel to your new rural idyll by car. If you are constructing a new building, consider using a brownfield site in an urban location close to housing, shops and good public transport links.**

PUT YOUR WORKPLACE NEAR A BUS STOP By locating your office in an area easily accessed by public transport you will reduce the need for people to drive to work, cutting emissions. If possible, choose a site within walking distance of a train station or reliable bus route.

CASE STUDY
VANCOUVER PARKS ITS CAR CULTURE

In Vancouver, Canada, the city has devised what it calls its EcoDensity project, which seeks to restrict urban sprawl and reduce the need for people to commute long distances to work. It encourages affordable housing and centres of business to be built side by side, and will guide all the city's future decisions on planning and development. The mayor of Vancouver, Sam Sullivan, says: 'Instead of building sprawling communities with automobile-based infrastructure, municipal governments must plan for the future by designing more dense and liveable neighbourhoods so that citizens are less dependent on cars.'

MOVE INTO AN ECO-OFFICE Save the hassle of building your own eco-office, or renovating an old, inefficient building, by relocating to a ready-made environmentally friendly office. The government passed regulations in 2006 for all new office buildings to produce less CO_2 emissions, and so any development built since then should be relatively green. Some, of course, go further. The Container City developments (**www.containercity.com**), for example, have been created using recycled shipping containers.

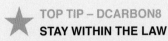

TOP TIP – DCARBON8
STAY WITHIN THE LAW

New EU law requires that if you're refitting, extending or relocating to a building over 1,000m², you need an Environmental Performance Certificate (EPC). EPCs grade a building on its carbon footprint, on a scale from a top end of A to a lowest rating of G. If your rating is closer to G than A, consider reducing your footprint, moving somewhere else or, if you're a tenant, negotiating a lower rent. Public buildings over 1,000m² must, by law, display this grade at the entrance. Visit **www.dcarbon8.com**.

Renovation

INSULATION, INSULATION, INSULATION It may not be as glamorous as installing a wind turbine or glinting solar panels on your roof, but if you only do one thing to make your building more energy efficient, insulate it. As much as 40% of the energy you use to create heat may be sailing straight out of your building through poorly insulated walls, windows and roofing. Across the country, millions of tonnes of CO_2 are being wasted every year because of poor insulation. For information on how to insulate your office, visit the National Energy Foundation website at www.nef.org.uk.

AVOID OZONE-DEPLETING CHEMICALS IN INSULATION

Don't counteract the environmental benefits of insulation by using materials full of hydrochlorofluorocarbons (HCFCs). Although an improvement on chlorofluorocarbons (CFCs), which were previously used in insulation, HCFCs still contribute to depleting the ozone layer. There are lots of eco-friendly alternatives you can use, such as cork, wool and even newspaper. For more information, visit **www.greenbuildingstore.co.uk**.

ON THE JOB Builders are renowned for many things, but being environmentally conscious is not usually one of them. However, working hard among the less-scrupulous merchants are thousands of eco-friendly builders, as well as surveyors, architects and other tradesmen. You can find many of them listed on the website of the Sustainable Building Association (**www.aecb.net**).

USE RECYCLED MATERIALS Look for reclaimed building materials such as bricks, radiators, hand basins or wooden floors. As well as reducing the environmental impact of your renovation, it also provides a market for second-hand goods, which encourages the recycling of materials within the building industry. Old materials are also often cheaper and of better quality than new materials. The website **www.salvo.co.uk** has a directory of suppliers you can trawl through.

INSTALL A CONDENSING BOILER Condensing boilers convert 88% of their fuel into heat, compared to only 72% for standard boilers. They contain an extra heat exchanger, so when the boiler works at peak efficiency the water vapour produced in the combustion process condenses back into liquid, releasing extra heat. This added efficiency will save you around 12% on your bills. Find out more at **www.nef.org.uk**.

IN (AND OUT) THROUGH THE WINDOW In terms of the energy efficiency of your building, windows are perhaps the single most important element. A standard single-glazed window can lose up to 14 times as much heat from a room as the same area of well-insulated wall. However, windows also let in heat and light from the sun, and in this way they can help to reduce a building's energy needs. Getting the right balance between these two factors is a tricky business, but the British Fenestration Ratings Council has come up with a helpful energy rating system that factors in both heat leakage and solar gain, as well as the efficiency of the materials used. It then gives every window a rating from a top grade of A to the lowest rating of G. All windows with a C rating and above are eligible to display the Energy Saving Trust's 'energy saving recommended' logo.

TIMBER VS PVC-U WINDOWS Put simply, double-glazed windows are generally more energy efficient than single-glazed windows. But don't think that is all you need to consider. Most double-glazing is made out of PVC. This is bad. The production and disposal of PVC-U windows leads to the release of highly poisonous chemicals that threaten the environment and human health. Most PVC-U windows are also not recyclable, so they need to be disposed of either in landfill or through a very inefficient incineration process. Despite perceptions that PVC-U windows are maintenance-free, they do break and when they do they are difficult to repair. The alternative – timber windows – are more easily repaired, can be produced from sustainable sources and are biodegradable. According to Greenpeace, timber windows are 'by far the best environmental choice'.

DOUBLE-GLAZED TIMBER: THE PERFECT SOLUTION As well as being better for the environment, timber windows also look nicer than PVC-U. However, they are usually single-glazed and energy inefficient. The ultimate solution to this conundrum is to find energy-efficient timber

windows. Eco Windows (**www.eco-windows.co.uk**) sells a wide range of double-glazed timber windows, and even mainstream manufacturers such as Everest are now starting to produce eco-friendly double-glazed timber windows.

STAY OFF THE SOLVENTS Many modern gloss paints can contain up to 50% solvents and volatile organic compounds (VOCs). This is dangerous stuff. The World Health Organisation says that decorators face a 40% increased chance of lung cancer as a result of continued exposure to these paints. So would you really want your office walls coated in them? Solvent paints also have a high product-to-waste ratio – every tonne of paint produced results in 30 tonnes of waste. Instead, use natural paints made from plant and mineral bases, such as those available at **www.ecosolutions.co.uk**, **www.auro.co.uk** or **www.thegreenshop.co.uk**.

DONATE YOUR TOOLS After all the building work is done, if you've got any tools left unwanted, donate them to Tools For Self-Reliance (**www.tfsr.org.uk**), a charity that will refurbish them and send them to tradespeople in Africa. It ships goods worth over £500,000 each year to communities in Tanzania, Zimbabwe, Uganda and Ghana. If you are based in Northern Ireland, the charity Tools For Solidarity (**www.toolsforsolidarity.org.uk**) does a similar thing.

Bathrooms

DUAL-ACTION LOOS **Every time an employee flushes a toilet at least eight litres of contaminated water are dumped into the sewage system. You do the maths, but depending on the number of employees you have, that's a lot of dirty water that needs treating. Not only that, but it costs you money. Of course, no one advocates asking your workers to use the loo less, but there are lots of ways to make your toilets more water efficient. The simplest solution is to install dual-flush loos that have the option of a half flush for**

those less messy deposits. Make sure the dual-flush facility is clear and easy to understand, however, or you might find it becomes inefficient and your employees end up flushing more than once, wasting even more water.

LOW-FLUSH LOOS   Even better than dual-flush loos are low-flush loos, such as the Ifo Cera ES4 from the Green Building Store (**www.greenbuildingstore.co.uk**), which are designed to work efficiently with less water in all circumstances.

TOP TIP – SURFERS AGAINST SEWAGE
THINK BEFORE YOU FLUSH!

Make sure all the toilets in your workplace have a dedicated bin in place, so non-flushable sanitary items don't end up causing pollution incidents. The toilet is not and should not be used as a wet bin, but millions of us continue to flush sanitary products like cotton bud sticks, tampons, tampon applicators, sanitary towels and condoms down the toilet instead of putting them in a bin. These sanitary products can and do cause blockages in the sewerage system, resulting in untreated sewage escaping into our seas and reducing water quality. For more information about how you can help surfers fight against sewage visit **www.sas.org.uk**.

FLUSH USING RAINWATER   Save water, and the energy needed to clean it and pump it into your office, by flushing your loos with rainwater. There are lots of modern systems available that will collect rainwater in an underground tank as it runs off your roof – so you don't have to leave a bucket outside the office's back door. For information on the various rainwater-harvesting systems, visit Renewable Energy UK at **www.reuk.co.uk/Collect-Rainwater.htm**.

INSTALL SPRAY TAPS   Taps left running or even dripping can waste huge amounts of water and energy – almost 3% of the UK's electricity is used for moving water around. To prevent waste, install spray taps or taps fitted with push-tops, or infrared controls, which can reduce water consumption by up to 50%.

USE SENSOR LIGHT SWITCHES It is unlikely that your office bathroom will be in constant use, unless you are a big firm. You could try putting up a sign asking staff to save energy by turning off the lights when they leave, and it may work. Alternatively, you could install sensor lights that sense when someone enters or leaves the room and turn on or off accordingly.

Outside

IF YOUR OFFICE HAS OUTSIDE SPACE, PLANT A GARDEN **An office garden brings with it many benefits. It encourages wildlife, such as birds and insects, and gives staff somewhere to sit and de-stress or eat their lunch. A garden can also help keep your office cool in summer and, if it includes trees, protect it from wind, keeping it warmer in winter. If you have managed to encourage your staff to use alternative means of transport to get to work (see chapter 13), you could be super-green and turn some of those redundant parking spaces into a garden.**

GREEN ON TOP Grow plants on your roof. It may sound like a wacky idea, but it is simple to do and has many environmental benefits. A green roof will insulate a building from heat loss in the winter and heat gain in the summer, reducing those costly energy bills. It will also help reduce pollution, particularly in urban areas. Green roofs can reduce rainwater run-off by at least 50%, contributing to urban drainage and flood alleviation schemes. They can also attract wildlife, particularly birds. The type of vegetation you grow on your roof needs to be carefully thought out, of course, and it is probably best to consult experts, such as Living Roofs (**www.livingroofs.org**), rather than getting out a ladder and some gardening gloves and attempting to do it yourself. If you do fancy a bit of roof gardening, however, The Green Roof Centre (**www.thegreenroofcentre.co.uk**) has a DIY guide you can download.

 TOP TIP – NATURE ENGLAND
GET MUCKY TO GET GREEN

Plant a low-impact, wildlife-friendly garden. By planting native trees and wildflowers you can encourage biodiversity and provide a relaxing place for employees on lunchbreaks. Collect rainwater in water butts and use it to water the garden. Generate quality compost for your grounds or garden from food waste generated in the office. You can set up compost caddies for ground coffee and teabags, while a small domestic-style compost bin can also be installed. Another option is to use wormeries. A wormery is an environmentally-friendly way to recycle food waste by converting it into quality compost. This is an excellent way to get staff involved in environmental activities while reducing the amount of waste generated from your office.

CASE STUDY
SCHOOLS IN JAPAN GET GREEN CURTAIN MAKEOVER

Hundreds of schools in Japan have been growing cucumbers in a bid to save energy. The huge plants, which are tended by schoolchildren during their break times, are grown right next to the school buildings and act as a shade, reducing the need for air conditioning. The moisture given off by the plants, which reach up to three floors in height, also helps reduce temperatures. The project has been so successful that it is now being copied by parents at home, and a City Hall in Tokushima has joined in, growing goya vegetables, which are similar to cucumbers. A professor from the Nippon Institute of Technology studied the project at one school and found it reduced the temperature in the building by up to 4°C.

USE SOLAR-POWERED SECURITY LIGHTS These lights charge up during the day when they're not needed and then at night they're fully powered and ready to light up if they sense any movement outside your building. Once installed, there is no electricity required and therefore no running costs. Just make sure you place them in a position where the sun will shine on them. For one of the many suppliers of these lights, visit **www.sunshinesolar.co.uk**.

DON'T TREAT FENCING WITH CREOSOTE Creosote dissolves in water and can then get through the soil to groundwater, where it takes years to break down. If you can, grow a hedge or build a wall from reclaimed bricks instead.

Moving on

OFFICE MOVE Moving office can be a very environmentally unfriendly event. All those big lorries,

plastic polywraps, cardboard boxes and office waste that you don't want to bring with you is dumped in black bin bags and carted off to landfill. Of course, there is another way. Start by asking your removal company about its environmental policy. If it doesn't have one, or you are not happy with it, find one that does. They do exist. Alexanders (www.alexandersremovals.co.uk) in London, for example, uses recycled packaging materials and offsets its carbon.

AVOID CARDBOARD BOXES The UK produces over eight million tonnes of cardboard for use in packaging every year. While cardboard is recyclable, it still requires a lot of energy and raw materials to produce all of those boxes. An eco-conscious removal firm will save waste by moving your things in reusable crates instead. If you do have to use cardboard boxes, buy recycled ones, or reuse any boxes you already have in your workplace – collect them in the weeks leading up to your move.

SPRING CLEANING Moving office is a chance to clear out all those unwanted items that have been building up on desks and in storerooms. But don't just throw them all in the bin. It may be more effort to recycle, but it will greatly reduce your impact on the environment. Set up separate bins for paper, cardboard, waste metals, plastic bottles and glass. Set aside unwanted electrical equipment and computers that still work to give to charity (see chapter 8). If sorting all this out is too much for you, try to find an eco-clearance company to do it for you, such as Becs (**www.ecobecs.co.uk**).

UPGRADE YOUR COMPUTERS Invest in a strong IT team that can upgrade your computers when they start to creak, rather than a team that just buys new ones every time something stops working. If every office in the UK upgraded its computers once rather than buying new ones, this would save about 2.5 million tonnes of fossil fuel.

GIVE UNWANTED FURNITURE TO CHARITY The charity Green-Works (**www.green-works.co.uk**) will collect your unwanted office furniture and pass it on at a low cost to charities, schools, community groups and small start-up businesses. It will take anything, from desks to coat stands, noticeboards and carpet tiles. Even if the furniture is in a poor condition, Green-Works will remanufacture it into something else, or recycle what it can't reuse.

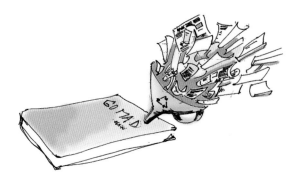

Find out more!

All the organisations mentioned in *Make a Difference at Work* are listed here – so make that phone call, send that email or write that letter!

Make a Difference at Work is all about interaction, so please let us know of any organisations or initiatives you feel should be mentioned in the book, as well as any new environmental tips. Send your idea by post or email and if we use your suggestion, we'll send you a free copy of the next edition of *Make a Difference at Work*!

Make a Difference Tips
Think Publishing Ltd
The Pall Mall Deposit
124-128 Barlby Road
London W10 6BL

Email editorial@thinkpublishing.co.uk.
Don't forget to include your address.

Contacts

AMAZING RECYCLED PRODUCTS
An American company specialising in innovative products made from a wide variety of recycled materials.
www.amazingrecycled.com

AMNESTY INTERNATIONAL
Worldwide movement of people campaigning for internationally recognised human rights.
17-25 New Inn Yard, London EC2A 3EA
• 020 7033 1500
www.amnesty.org

ANITARODDICK.COM
Body Shop founder campaigns on environmental and humanitarian issues.
www.anitaroddick.com

ARCANIA GREEN TECHNOLOGY SPECIALISTS
The first UK company to offer services powered by 100% solar power.
www.arcania.co.uk

ASSOCIATION FOR ENVIRONMENT CONSCIOUS BUILDING
UK's leading independent environmental building trade organisation.
PO Box 32, Llandysul SA44 5ZA
• 0845 4569773
www.aecb.net

AURO UK
Organic paints. Cheltenham Road, Bisley, Nr Stroud, Gloucestershire GL6 7BX
• 01452 772020
www.auroorganic.co.uk

AVEDA
For environmentally friendly hair, skin, makeup and lifestyle products.
www.aveda.co.uk

BAG IT AND BIN IT
National water industry-led campaign promoting responsible disposal of discarded personal products.
www.bagandbin.org

BEANIES WHOLEFOODS
Specialists in quality organic foods.
205-207 Crookes Valley Road, Sheffield S10 1BA
• 0114 268 1662
www.beanieswholefoods.co.uk

BEAUTY NATURALS
High-quality, natural health and beauty products.
• 0845 094 0400
www.beautynaturals.com

BEAUTY WITHOUT CRUELTY
An international educational charitable trust for animal rights.
www.bwcindia.org

BENFIELD ATT
Information, help and materials for self-build kit-houses and DIY homes.
• 01291 437050
www.adtimtec.com

BEST FOOT FORWARD
A company set up to assist individuals and organisations to become environmentally sustainable.
The Future Centre, 9 Newtec Place, Magdalen Road, Oxford OX4 1RE
• 01865 250818
www.bestfootforward.com

BICYCLE BEANO
Offers cycling tours of the Welsh countryside, combined with quality accommodation and vegetarian cuisine.
• 01982 560471
www.bicycle-beano.co.uk

BIO REGIONAL DEVELOPMENT GROUP
A group founded on the ideal of local production for local needs, that promotes sustainable development. BedZED Centre, Helios Road, Wallington, Surrey SM6 7BZ
• 020 8404 4880
www.bioregional.com

BODY SHOP INTERNATIONAL PLC

International retail chain renowned for
its environmentally friendly and naturally
inspired beauty products.
www.thebodyshop.com

BOYCOTTBUSH

This site is where *Ethical Consumer* charts the
campaigners' progress and lists the brands for
consumers to avoid.
www.boycottbush.net

BRITISH ASSOCIATION FOR FAIR TRADE SHOPS

A network of independent Fair Trade or
World Shops, aiming to promote Fairtrade
retail in the UK.
13 Spring Gardens Place, Cardiff CF24 1QY
• 07882 680113
www.bafts.org.uk

BRITISH GLASS MANUFACTURERS CONFEDERATION

Promotes glass as the leading choice
for containers.
www.britglass.co.uk

BRITISH RED CROSS

For your nearest British Red Cross shop.
UK Office, 44 Moorfields,
London EC2Y 9AL
• 0870 170 7000
www.redcross.org.uk

BRITISH TRUST FOR CONSERVATION VOLUNTEERS

An organisation that works with volunteers
to bring about positive environmental change.
Sedum House, Mallard Way, Potteric Carr,
Doncaster DN4 8DB
• 01302 388 888
www.btcv.org

BRITISH WIND ENERGY ASSOCIATION

Aims to promote wind energy in the UK.
• 020 7689 1960
www.bwea.com/about/index.html

BUSINESS IN THE ENVIRONMENT

Movement of over 700 UK companies to
improve their positive impact on society.
137 Shepherdess Walk, London N1 7RQ
• 020 7566 8650
www.bitc.org.uk

BUY NOTHING DAY

A day celebrating simple living and
no spending.
www.buynothingday.co.uk

BUY RECYCLED

Guide to products available in the UK
containing recycled materials.
• 0845 456 7689
www.bynature.co.uk

CAFÉDIRECT

Sells fairly traded tea, coffee and cocoa that
provides producer partners with a living wage.
• 020 7490 9520
www.cafedirect.co.uk

CAMPAIGN TO PROTECT RURAL ENGLAND

Campaigns for the protection and
enhancement of the countryside.
CPRE national office: 128 Southwark Street,
London SE1 0SW • 020 7981 2800
www.cpre.org.uk

CAMPAIGNS OF THE NATIONAL LABOUR COMMITTEE

Promotes and defends workers' rights on
a global scale.
National Labor Committee
75 Varick St., Suite 1500, New York, NY
10013, USA • +1 212 242 3002
www.nlcnet.org

CANBY

Provides jute bags and environmentally
friendly packaging.
Canby Ltd, 27 Park End Street, Oxford
OX1 1HU • 0845 277 0122
www.canby.co.uk

CARBON TRUST

Promotes the development of low carbon
technologies to support the transition to a
low-carbon technology in the UK.
Carbon Trust, 8th Floor,
3 Clement's Inn, London WC2A 2AZ
• 0800 085 2005
www.thecarbontrust.co.uk

CARBONNEUTRAL COMPANY

Plants trees to help neutralise carbon
dioxide emissions.
Bravington House, 2 Bravington Walk,
Regent Quarter, Kings Cross, London
N1 9AF • 020 7833 6000
www.carbonneutral.com

CARPLUS

Car-sharing projects.
• 0113 234 9299
www.carplus.org.uk

THE CARTRIDGE COMPANY

Collects and delivers cartridges to offices and work places.
• 0800 08 08 08
http://thecartridge.co.uk

CARTRIDGES 4 CHARITY

Funds small charities by recycling printer cartridges and mobile phones.
www.cartridges4charity.co.uk

CASH FOR CANS

Promotes local-level aluminium recycling in the UK and abroad, offering incentives to individuals and organisations.
www.thinkcans.com

CENTRE FOR ALTERNATIVE TECHNOLOGY

Environmental charity that aims to inspire, inform and enable people to live more sustainably.
• 01654 705950
www.cat.org.uk

CENTRE FOR SUSTAINABLE URBAN AND REGIONAL FEATURES

Promotes urban regeneration and renewal
• 0161 295 4018
www.surf.salford.ac.uk

CHANGING PLACES

Tackles the legacy of post-industrial decay to breathe new life into derelict and neglected land.
www.changingplaces.org.uk

CHARITY CARDS

Provides a selection of charity cards for Christmas and other celebrations.
• 0191 261 6263
www.charitycards.co.uk
www.christmas-cards.org.uk

CHARITY COMMISSION

A government organisation aiming to increase public confidence in the integrity of charities in England and Wales.
• 0845 3000 218
www.charity-commission.gov.uk

CHILDREN'S SCRAPSTORE

Recycles clean and safe waste products to create resources for children's art and play activities.
The Proving House, Sevier Street, St Werburghs, Bristol BS2 9LB
• 0117 908 5644
www.childrensscrapstore.co.uk

CHOOSE CLIMATE

Calculates the cost of your flight to the environment.
www.chooseclimate.org

CLIMATE ARK

Offers news and information on climate change and renewable energy.
www.climateark.org

COMMUNITY COMPOSTING NETWORK

Provides advice and supports community composting projects across the UK.
• 0114 258 0483
www.communitycompost.org

COMMUNITY RECYCLING NETWORK

A membership organisation promoting community-based sustainable waste management. • 0117 942 0142
www.crn.org.uk

COMMUNITY REPAINT

A scheme to collect and distribute paint to people who can't afford it.
www.communityrepaint.org.uk

COMPUTER AID INTERNATIONAL

Charity that refurbishes computers from the UK for reuse in developing countries.
• 020 8361 5540
www.computeraid.org

COMPUTERS FOR CHARITY

A voluntary organisation that campaigns to improve access to IT for community groups, through the recycling of computers.
• 01288 361199
www.computersforcharity.org.uk

CONFRONTING COMPANIES USING SHAREHOLDER POWER

Handbook for socially conscious investors.
www.foe.org/international/shareholder

CONSERVATREE
Promotes recycled paper products within the paper industry.
www.conservatree.com

CO-OPERATIVE BANK
Ethically guided banking facilities, encouraging business customers to invest in environmentally conscious companies. Head Office, PO Box 101, 1 Balloon Street, Manchester M60 4EP • 0845 600 6000
www.cooperativebank.co.uk

CORPORATE WATCH
Investigates corporate crime and monitors corporate power.
16B Cherwell Street, Oxford OX4 1BG
• 01865 791391
www.corporatewatch.org.uk

CORPWATCH
Counters corporate-led globalisation through education, networking and activism.
www.corpwatch.org

CRITICAL MASS RIDES WORLDWIDE
Organised worldwide group of cyclists who resist the problem of car culture.
www.urban75.com/Action/critical.html

CTC
A one-stop shop for cyclists. PO Box 868, Crawley RH10 9WW • 0870 873 0061
www.ctc.org.uk

CULTIVATING COMMUNITIES
Provides information on supporting local agricultural communities.
www.cuco.org.uk

DCARBON8 LTD
Carbon and sustainability consultants specialising in carbon measurement and reduction, supply chain management, corporate sustainability and development.
70 Cowcross Street, London EC1M 6EL
• 020 7250 1551
www.dcarbon8.com

DEODORANT STONE (UK)
Range of natural body deodorants that do not contain aluminium chlorohydrate and are not tested on animals. Caer Delyn, Dolgran, Pencader, Carmarthenshire SA39 9BX
• 01559 384856
www.deodorant-stone.co.uk

DO-IT-YOURSELF NETWORK
A site dedicated to DIY information, including tips on personal recycling projects and composting.
www.diynet.com

DOVES FARM FOODS
Gluten-free organic food manufacturer. Salisbury Road, Hungerford, Berkshire RG17 0RF
www.dovesfarm.co.uk

DRIVE ELECTRIC
The electric vehicle specialists.
• 0844 88 44 787
www.drivelectric.com

EARTHSCAN
Publishers of books on the environment and sustainable development.
• 020 7387 8558
www.earthscan.co.uk

EBAY
Online auction for second-hand goods.
www.ebay.co.uk

EBONY SOLUTIONS
Sells fuel made from cooking oil.
www.ebony-solutions.co.uk

ECO CLOTHING
01604 621531
www.ecofair.co.uk

ECO SALVAGE
Removes abandoned cars and derelict equipment.
www.ecosalvage.com

ECO-SCHOOLS
Aims to get everyone in a school community involved in improving the environment.
www.ecoschools.org.uk

ECOLOGY BUILDING SOCIETY
A building society dedicated to improving the environment by promoting sustainable housing and communities.
• 0845 674 5566
www.ecology.co.uk

ECOS ORGANIC PAINTS
Makers of odourless, solvent-free gloss and emulsion paints.
• 01524 852371
www.ecospaints.com

ECOTEC
Products aimed at improving car fuel consumption. • 01844 212939
www.ecotekplc.com

ECOTOPIA
Supplies a great range of eco-friendly, ethical, sustainable and natural products.
www.ecotopia.co.uk

ECOTRICITY
The world's first green energy company.
www.ecotricity.com

ECOVER UK LTD
Manufactures environmentally friendly detergents and cleaning products.
www.ecover.com

ECOZONE
A range of eco-friendly products for use in and around the home.
www.ecozone.co.uk

ELECTRIC CAR ASSOCIATION
Electric cars, conversions and components.
• 01823 480196
www.avt.uk.com

ENERGY SAVING TRUST
Promoting sustainable and efficient uses of energy. • 020 7222 0101
www.energysavingtrust.org.uk

ENERGY STAR
Provides information on energy saving and the energy-saving star rating.
www.energystar.gov

ENVIRONMENT AGENCY
Information on energy rating schemes.
• 08708 506 506
www.environment-agency.gov.uk

ENVIRONMENTAL INVESTIGATION AGENCY (EIA)
An international organisation committed to investigating and exposing environment-related crimes.62/63 Upper Street, London N1 0NY • 020 7354 7960
www.eia-international.org

ENVIRONMENTAL MOBILE CONTROL
Provides recycling solutions for surplus mobile phone equipment. • 01283 516259
www.emc-recycle.com

ENVIRONMENTAL TRANSPORT ASSOCIATION (ETA)
Motoring organisation campaigning for a sustainable transport system.
• 0845 389 1010
www.eta.co.uk

ETHICAL CONSUMER
Alternative consumer organisation researching the environmental and social records of the companies behind the brand names.
Unit 21, 41 Old Birley Street, Manchester M15 5RF • 0161 226 2929
www.ethicalconsumer.org

ETHICAL INVESTMENT RESEARCH SERVICE (EIRIS)
Provides research into corporate behaviour for ethical investors.
80-84 Bondway, London SW8 1SF
• 020 7840 5700
www.eiris.org

ETHICAL JUNCTION
Information on ethical organisations and ethically made products.
112 Lyndhurst Road, Ashurst, Southampton, Hampshire SO40 7AU
• 023 80293763
www.ethicaljunction.org

ETHICAL TRADING INITIATIVE
An alliance of companies, NGOs and trade union organisations working together to promote ethical trade.
www.ethicaltrade.org

ETHICAL WARES
Ethical mail order company run by vegans who trade without exploiting animals, humans or the wider environment.
www.ethicalwares.com

EUROPA
Website of the European Union.
www.europa.eu.int

EXPERIENCE CORPS
Encourages volunteering in local communities near and far.
www.experiencecorps.co.uk

FAIRTRADE FOUNDATION
Promotes Fairtrade and campaigns to encourage the growth of global Fairtrade.
www.fairtrade.org.uk

FIELD STUDIES COUNCIL

An educational charity committed to teaching environmental issues. Montford Bridge, Preston Montford, Shrewsbury, Shropshire SY4 1HW • 01743 852100
www.field-studies-council.org

FIRST GIVING

Processes charity donations online.
www.firstgiving.com

FOOD DOCTOR

Independent professional advice on nutrition and health.
• 020 7792 6700
www.thefooddoctor.com

FOOD STANDARDS AGENCY

Valuable information on food labelling, organic food, food safety and GM crops.
www.foodstandards.gov.uk

FREE WHEELERS

Campaigns to reduce pollution by reducing car usage.
www.freewheelers.com

FRESH FOOD COMPANY

Organic fruit, vegetables, meat, fish, wine and bread, and organic recipes.
www.freshfood.co.uk

FRESH WATER FILTER COMPANY

Water filters for the home.
• 020 8558 7495
www.freshwaterfilter.com

FRIENDS OF CONSERVATION

Funds international community conservation projects and works with the travel industry to promote sustainable tourism.
• 020 7603 5024
www.foc-uk.com

FRIENDS OF THE EARTH

A national environmental pressure group with local groups who campaign on environmental issues. • 020 7490 1555 (information service: 0800 581 051)
www.foe.org.uk

FRIENDS OF THE EARTH – SCOTLAND

www.foe-scotland.org.uk

FRIENDS OF THE EARTH – WALES

www.foe.co.uk/cymru

FRIENDS PROVIDENT

Ethical financial products and services.
• 0870 607 1352
www.friendsprovident.co.uk

FURNITURE RE-USE NETWORK

Promotes the reuse of furniture and household effects for the alleviation of hardship. 48-54 West Street, St Philips, Bristol BS2 0BL • 0117 954 3571
www.frn.org.uk

FUTURE HEATING LTD

All types of heating installation, including solar. 208 Chase Side, Enfield, Middlesex EN2 0QX • 020 8351 9360
www.future-heating.co.uk

GET ETHICAL

Shopping portal that promotes ethical shopping and supports social enterprises in the UK.
www.getethical.com

GLOBAL WITNESS

Campaigns to end the links between natural resource exploitation and conflict and corruption. PO Box 6042, London N19 5WP
• 020 7272 6731
www.globalwitness.org

GOOD ENERGY

Supplies renewable energy products to homes and businesses.
Good Energy, Monkton Reach, Monkton Hill, Chippenham, Wiltshire SN15 1EE
• 01249 766090
www.good-energy.co.uk

GOSSYPIUM

An ethical eco-cotton store that manufactures fairly traded clothing.
Unit 1, Shepherd Industrial Estate, Brooks Road, Lewes BN7 2BY
• 0870 850 9953
www.gossypium.co.uk

GREEN BATTERIES

Promotes the use of rechargeable batteries.
www.greenbatteries.com

GREEN BUILDING STORE

Safe, sustainable building products.
Heath House Mill, Heath House Lane, Bolster Moor, West Yorkshire HD7 4JW
• 01484 461705
www.greenbuildingstore.co.uk

GREEN CHOICES
A guide to greener living.
www.greenchoices.org

GREEN CHRONICLE
Information on growing, buying, eating and living organically.
www.greenchronicle.com

GREEN ENERGY
Encourages sustainable and green sources of energy.
The National Energy Foundation,
Davy Avenue, Knowlhill, Milton Keynes
MK5 8NG • 01908 665555
www.nef.org.uk/greenenergy

GREEN FIBRES
Organic clothing and home products made from organic cotton, linen, hemp, wool and silk, with a wedding list service.
www.greenfibres.com

GREEN FUTURES
A magazine on environmental solutions and sustainable futures published by Forum for the Future.
www.greenfutures.org.uk

GREEN GUIDES
Database of organic, eco-friendly and ethical businesses and organisations.
Markham Publishing, 31 Regal Road,
Weasenham Lane Industrial Estate,
Wisbech, Cambridgeshire PE13 2RQ
• 01945 461452
www.greenguide.co.uk

GREENMATTERS
Site designed to help busy people live a greener life.
www.greenmatters.com

GREENPEACE
Campaigns to expose global environmental problems and their causes.
www.greenpeace.org

GREEN PRICES
Compares products and prices of green energy suppliers in Europe.
www.greenprices.com

GREEN STATIONERY COMPANY
Environmentally friendly stationery products. Studio 1, 114 Walcot Street,
Bath BA1 5BG • 01225 480556
www.greenstat.co.uk

GREEN WORKS
Redundant office equipment for schools, charities, community groups and start-up businesses.
• 0845 230 2231
www.green-work.co.uk

GROUNDWORK
Environmental regeneration charity working for sustainable development in some of the UK's poorest communities.
Lockside, 5 Scotland Street,
Birmingham B1 2RR
• 0121 236 8565
www.groundwork.org.uk

HEALTHY HOUSE
Products for a healthy environment, at home and in the office. The Old Co-Op, Lower Street, Ruscombe, Stroud,
Gloucestershire GL6 6BU
• 01453 752216
www.healthy-house.co.uk

HIPPO THE WATER SAVER
Water-saving device for toilet cisterns.
• 01989 766667 (order line)
www.hippo-the-watersaver.co.uk

HONESTY COSMETICS
Wide range of skin and hair products, suitable for vegetarians and vegans.
• 01629 814888
www.honestycosmetics.co.uk

H2OUSE
Information and advice on how to use water efficiently.
www.h2ouse.org

IMPACT INITIATIVES
Information on how to do your bit for your community.
www.impact-initiatives.org.uk

IMPROVEMENT AND DEVELOPMENT AGENCY (IDEA)
An agency promoting the involvement of local authorities in Local Agenda 21.
• 020 7296 6600
www.idea.gov.uk

INSTITUTE OF SOCIAL AND ETHNIC ACCOUNTABILITY
Enhancing the performance of companies' sustainable development records.
• 020 7549 0400
www.accountability.org.uk

227

INTERMEDIATE TECHNOLOGY DEVELOPMENT GROUP (ITDG)

Advocates sustainable use of technology to reduce poverty in developing countries.
• 01926 634400
www.itdg.org

KINETICS

Specialists in folding and electric bikes.
• 0141 942 2552
www.kbikes.co.uk

KINGFISHER NATURAL TOOTHPASTE

Producing natural toothpaste with no added preservatives or colourings.
• 01603 630484
www.kingfishertoothpaste.com

LIFTSHARE COMMUNITY SCHEME

Car-sharing scheme.
www.liftshare.org

LOCAL EXCHANGE TRADING SYSTEM (LETSLINK)

Local community-based networks allowing people to exchange goods and services with each other without the need for money.
• 020 7607 7852
www.letslinkuk.org

LONDON CYCLING CAMPAIGN

Campaigns to make London a world-class cycling city.
• 020 7234 9310
www.lcc.org.uk

LOW IMPACT LIVING INITIATIVE

Promotes harmonious ways of living with the environment.
• 01296 714184
www.lowimpact.org

LP GAS ASSOCIATION

Commercial propane and butane gas.
www.lpga.co.uk

MAKING COSMETICS

How to make cosmetics at home from natural and manufactured raw materials.
www.makingcosmetics.com

MAKINGYOURCOSMETICS.COM

For recipes and information on ingredients.
www.makeyourcosmetics.com

MAN IN SEAT 61

Journey advice from a man who has travelled the world by rail and sea.
www.seat61.com

MERCY CORPS

Alleviating suffering and poverty by helping people build secure communities.
www.mercycorps.com

MILLENNIUM VOLUNTEERS PROGRAMME

An initiative for people aged 16-24, offering the chance to build on skills and use time more constructively.
27 Ardwick Green North, Manchester M12 6FZ• 0161 274 3299
www.gmyn.co.uk/v/

MOUNTAIN BIKING UK

Info on mountain biking in the UK.
• 01225 442244
www.mbuk.com

NATIONAL ASSOCIATION OF PAPER MERCHANTS (NAPM)

The trade association representing the interests of UK paper merchants.
PO Box 2850, Nottingham NG5 2WW
• 0115 8412129
www.napm.org.uk

NATIONAL CENTRE FOR BUSINESS AND SUSTAINABILITY

A consultancy set up to help organisations improve their sustainability.
www.thencbs.co.uk

NATIONAL ENERGY FOUNDATION

A UK charity that provides free advice on energy efficiency and renewable energy.
The National Centre, Davy Avenue, Knowlhill, Milton Keynes MK5 8NG
• 01908 665555
www.nef.org.uk

NATIONAL RECYCLING FORUM

A guide to products that contain recycled materials.
www.recycledproducts.org.uk

NATIONAL SKI AREAS ASSOCIATION

Promotes efforts to reduce carbon dioxide and other heat-trapping emissions using wind-powered ski lifts and car-pooling.
www.nsaa.org

NATURAL CLOTHING

Offers a range of natural clothing
and products.
• 0845 345 0498
www.naturalclothing.co.uk

NATURAL COLLECTION

Online catalogue with a range of eclectic,
unusual, useful and interesting products
chosen to contribute to a better world.
• 0845 3677 001
www.naturalcollection.com

NATURAL ECO TRADING

Environmentally friendly household
cleaning products.
• 01892 616871
www.greenbrands.co.uk

NATURAL RESOURCES DEFENSE COUNCIL

An environmental action organisation.
40 West 20th Street New York,
NY 10011, USA • +1 212 727 2700
www.nrdc.org

NATURE SAVE – POLICIES LIMITED

Provides ethical insurance policies.
58 Fore Street, Totnes TQ9 5RU
• 01803 864390
www.naturesave.co.uk

NEW ECONOMICS FOUNDATION

Promotes solutions to social, environmental
and economic problems.
3 Jonathan Street, London SE11 5NH
• 020 7820 6300
www.neweconomics.org

NOT TOO PRETTY

Information on cosmetics and associated
products that contain dangerous phthalates.
www.safecosmetics.org

OFFICES OF WATER SERVICES

England and Wales's sewage and water
industry's regulator.
• 0121 625 1300
www.ofwat.gov.uk

OIL BANK

Find the location of your nearest oil bank
to recycle old oil and filters.
• 08708 506 506
www.oilbankline.org.uk

ONLINE UK CHARITY ORGANISATIONS AND SHOPS

Provides information on a selection of
UK charities.
www.avoidtherush.co.uk/shopping/2005/
charities.htm

ORGANICA J

A company offering a collection of
organic, GM-free products, from clothing
to healthcare.
• 01330 850257
www.organicaj.co.uk

ORGANIC CONSUMERS' ASSOCIATION

A non-profit organisation campaigning
for food safety, organic agriculture, Fairtrade
and environmental sustainability.
• +1 218 226 4164
www.organicconsumers.org

ORGANIC FOOD, UK

Anything and everything you want to
know about organic food.
www.organicfood.co.uk

OXFAM

A relief and campaign organisation
committed to finding lasting solutions to
poverty and suffering around the world.
• 0870 333 2700
www.oxfam.org.uk

PAPER BACK

Supplier of recycled paper. • 020 8980 5580
www.paperback.coop

PHONE CO-OP

A telecommunications provider that takes
an ethical and environmentally responsible
approach to business.
• 0845 458 9070
www.phonecoop.org.uk

POLYMER REPROCESSORS LIMITED

Developing recycling techniques in the
plastics industry.
• 0151 707 3684
www.polymer-reprocessors.co.uk

POWABYKE

A company offering electric bikes as an
eco-friendly alternative to cars.
• 01225 443737
www.powabyke.com

POWERPLUS

A company specialising in fuel-saving and emission-reduction technology..

www.powerplus.be

PRELOVED

A website allowing you to buy and sell second-hand items.

www.preloved.co.uk

PURE H2O

A water purification company that provides water systems.

www.pureh2o.co.uk

PURE ORGANICS LIMITED

Producers of organic food.
• 01980 626263

www.organics.org

QUADRIS ENVIRONMENTAL INVESTMENTS

Runs socially responsible investment funds.
• 01483 756800

www.quadris.co.uk

RAMBLERS' ASSOCIATION

Works for walkers across England, Scotland and Wales.
• 020 7339 8500

www.ramblers.org.uk

RECLAIM THE STREETS

For information on street-reclaiming action around the world.

www.rts.gn.apc.org

RECOUP

Works with retailers, local authorities and businesses to successfully recycle plastics.
• 01733 390021

www.recoup.org

RE-CYCLE

Collects and donates second-hand bicycles to communities in developing countries.
• 01206 863111

www.re-cycle.org

RECYCLE MORE

Provides information on recycling in the UK, in homes, businesses and schools.
• 0845 068 2572

www.recycle-more.co.uk

RECYCLE NOW

Provides information on how to recycle rubbish around the UK.

www.recyclenow.com

RECYCLED PAPER SUPPLIES

Provides stationery products, including recycled paper, card and envelopes.
• 01676 533832

www.recycled-paper.co.uk or
www.rps.gn.apc.org

RECYCLING OF USED PLASTICS

Promotes plastic recycling in the UK.
• 01733 390021

www.recoup.org

REEL FURNITURE

Eco-friendly wooden furniture for home, garden and conservatory.
• 01953 457247

www.reelfurniture.co.uk

RE-FORM FURNITURE

Furniture made from 100% recycled materials. • 01209 890084

www.re-formfurniture.co.uk

REMARKABLE

Everyday items produced from recycled or sustainable sources. • 01905 769999

www.remarkable.co.uk

RESOURCE FUTURES

Provides specialist waste management solutions for a huge range of clients – from private sector companies to community organisations.
CREATE Centre, Smeaton Road, Bristol BS1 6XN • 0117 930 4355

www.resourcefutures.co.uk

RESPONSIBLETRAVEL.COM

Promotes eco-tourism holidays in over 110 countries, designed to benefit tourists, hosts and the environment.

www.responsibletravel.com

RESURGENCE

Ground-breaking magazine publishing articles on the cutting edge of current thinking, promoting creativity, ecology, spirituality and frugality.
Ford House, Hartland, Bideford, Devon EX39 6EE • 01237 441 293

www.resurgence.org

REUZE

A site about where, what and how to recycle in the UK.

www.reuze.co.uk

SALVO

Suppliers of vintage or antique building materials.

www.salvo.co.uk

SAVAWATT

Promotes the sensible use of electricity.
• +44 (0)24 7699 8569

www.savawatt.com

SAVE-A-CUP

Offers a recycling service.
• 01494 510167

www.save-a-cup.co.uk

SAVE OR DELETE

Campaigns to protect the world's forests from total destruction (see Greenpeace).

www.saveordelete.com

SAVE WASTE AND PROSPER (SWAP)

An environmental consultant that deals with sustainable management.
• 0113 243 8777

www.swap-web.co.uk

SCRIB

Steel Can Recycling Information Bureau. Everything you need know about can recycling. c/o Corus Steel Packaging Recycling, Trostre Works, Llanelli, Carmarthenshire SA14 9SD
• 01554 712632

www.scrib.org

SELECT SOLAR

Specialists in solar panels.
• 01793 752032

www.selectsolar.co.uk

SHARED INTEREST SOCIETY

A cooperative lending society, offering ethical investment in fair trade with developing countries. • 0845 840 9100

www.shared-interest.com

SMARTWOOD

Provides information about recycled wood products and runs a wood certification scheme. • +1 802-434-5491

www.smartwood.org

SMILE.CO.UK

Environmentally aware online bank.

www.smile.co.uk

SOAP KITCHEN

Provides a selection of hand-made natural toiletries and soaps.
• 01805 622944

www.thesoapkitchen.co.uk

SOIL ASSOCIATION

A campaigning and certification organisation for organic food and farming.
• 0117 314 5000

www.soilassociation.org.uk

SOLA LIGHTING LTD

Providers of energy-efficient daylight solutions for new or existing homes and businesses.
• 0845 458 0101

www.solalighting.com

SOLAR ENERGY ALLIANCE

Information and advice on solar-powered energy.
• 01502 515532

www.gosolar.u-net.com

SPIRIT OF NATURE LTD

Offers natural and environmentally friendly products, including organic clothing, natural skin care, and eco-household products.
• 0870 725 9885

www.spiritofnature.co.uk

SUMA

Wholesalers of organic, vegetarian, vegan and ethical foods.
• 01422 313845

www.suma.coop

SURFERS AGAINST SEWAGE

SAS campaigns for clean, safe recreational water, free from sewage effluents, toxic chemicals, nuclear waste and marine litter.
• 01872 555950

www.sas.org.uk

SUSTRANS (SAFE ROUTES TO SCHOOLS INFORMATION TEAM)

A sustainable transport charity that campaigns for a reduction in motor traffic and its adverse effects.
• 0845 113 0065

www.sustrans.org.uk

TEARFUND

Works for the elimination of global poverty – including campaigns on injustice, unfair trade and landmines.
• 0845 355 8355
www.tearfund.org

TIMBER RESEARCH DEVELOPMENT ASSOCIATION

An internationally recognised body dealing with the specification and use of timber and wood products.
TRADA, Stocking Lane, Hughenden Valley, High Wycombe HP14 4ND
• 01494 569600
www.trada.co.uk

TIMEBANK

A national organisation campaigning to raise awareness of the importance of giving time and volunteering.
2nd Floor, Downstream Building, 1 London Bridge, London SE1 9BG
• 0845 456 1668
www.timebank.org.uk

TOMS OF MAINE

Creates natural toothpaste and other products using ingredients from nature.
PO Box 1873, Salisbury SP4 6WZ
www.tomsofmaine.com

TOOLS FOR SELF RELIANCE

Works with local organisations in Africa to provide tools and training. TFSR, Southampton SO40 7GY
• 02380 869697
www.tfsr.org.uk

TOURISM CONCERN

A membership organisation campaigning for ethical and fair-traded tourism.
Stapleton House, 277-281 Holloway Road, London N7 8HN
• 020 7133 3330
www.tourismconcern.org.uk

TRIODOS BANK

A European ethical bank, financing initiatives that deliver social, environmental and cultural benefits. • 0117 973 9339
www.triodos.co.uk

U REFILL TONER LTD

Provides DIY toner refill kits.
• 0121 693 2644
www.refilltoner.com

UK COMPUTER RECYCLING

An environmentally friendly computer disposal service throughout Great Britain.
www.rdc.co.uk

UNITED NATIONS ENVIRONMENT PROGRAMME (UNEP)

UNEP DTIE, United Nations Avenue, Gigiri, PO Box 30552, 00100, Nairobi, Kenya
www.uneptie.org

UNICEF

United Nations programme to promote health, education, equality and protection for every child.
Africa House, 64-78 Kingsway WC2B 6NB
• 020 7405 5592
www.unicef.org

USHOPUGIVE

An online retail outlet that donates a percentage of what you spend to a charity of your choice, without you paying extra.
www.ushopugive.com

USWITCH

A company that helps customers take advantage of the lowest prices on gas, electricity, home phones and digital TVs from a range of suppliers.
111 Buckingham Palace Road London SW1 0SR • 0800 404 7908
www.uswitch.com

VOLUNTEER DEVELOPMENT NORTHERN IRELAND

A Northern Ireland charity providing support and advice to local volunteer agencies. 129 Ormeau Road, Belfast BT7 1SH • 02890 236100
www.volunteering-ni.org

VOLUNTEER DEVELOPMENT SCOTLAND

A Scottish charity providing support and advice to local volunteer agencies.
Volunteer Development Scotland, Stirling Enterprise Park, Stirling FK7 7RP
• 01786 479593
www.vds.org.uk

VOLUNTEER DEVELOPMENT WALES

A Welsh charity providing support and advice to local volunteer agencies.
www.wcva.org.uk

VOLUNTEERING ENGLAND

A UK charity providing support and
advice to local volunteer agencies.
www.volunteering.org.uk

VOLUNTEERING IRELAND

An Irish charity providing support and
advice to local volunteer agencies.
Coleraine House, Coleraine Street,
Dublin 7, Republic of Ireland
• +353 1 872 2622
www.volunteeringireland.com

WASTEAWARE

Household waste and recycling information.
www.wasteaware.org.uk

WASTECONNECT

An online database for searching local
recycling points in the UK.
www.wasteconnect.co.uk

WASTE EXCHANGE DIRECTORY
TELEPHONE DIRECTORY
RECYCLING SCHEME

• 02380 236806
www.integra.org.uk/wastedirectory

WASTE ONLINE

For information on how to dispose of
batteries and other waste.
www.wasteonline.org.uk

WASTE WATCH

An organisation that promotes and
encourages waste reduction, reuse and
recycling. 56-64 Leonard Street, London
EC2A 4LT • 020 7549 0300
www.wastewatch.org.uk

WATER AID

A charity working in Africa and Asia to
improve water infrastructure, and provide
sanitation and hygiene education.
47-49 Durham Street, London SE11 5JD
• 020 7793 4500
www.wateraid.org.uk

WHALE AND DOLPHIN
CONSERVATION SOCIETY (WDCS)

Working for the protection of whales,
dolphins and their environment worldwide.
• 0870 870 5001
www.wdcs.org

WILDFOWL AND WETLANDS TRUST

An organisation to research and protect
wildfowl and their habitats.
WWT Slimbridge, Gloucestershire GL2 7BT
• 01453 891900
www.wwt.org.uk

THE WILDLIFE TRUSTS

A wealth of information about wildlife and
our environment.
The Kiln, Waterside, Mather Road,
Newark, Nottinghamshire NG24 1WT
• 0870 036 7711
www.wildlifetrusts.org

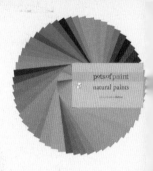

pots of paint

We sell a range of natural paints - **pots of** paint which now come in 50 delicious colours. We only use natural ingredients with no dangerous volatile organic compounds (VOCs) or synthetic solvents. This means no harmful emissions, no environmental pollution, they are breathable on walls and can withstand the daily wear and tear of office life. They have a pleasant smell, and a beautiful surface texture… Good design, naturally.

Please see our web for further details or give us a call for a hand painted swatch.